MW01710566

JONATHAN, DO YOU KNOW ME?

FROM LOSS OF A CHILD TO SPIRITUAL AWAKENING

VINCE LEITAO

This book is not intended as a substitute for the medical advice of physicians. The reader should regularly consult a physician in matters relating to health and particularly with respect to any symptoms that may require diagnosis or medical attention.

First edition published on December 23, 2015 by:
Vince Leitao
145 Royal Crest Court, #4
Unionville, ON L4C 9N9 Canada

ISBN: 978-0-9949509-0-1

The green background colour of the book is a dedication to increasing awareness of liver and bile duct cancer.

IN SUPPORT OF

SickKids®

Dedication

Jonathan, I dedicate this book to the love among us, to you and your memory.

For sixteen years, eight months and thirteen days, you brought joy and meaning to my earthly journey. May you be part of the glory and brilliance of God our Creator and reflect that glory and brilliance now and for eternity. I miss you and await the moment when I too will share in the glory and brilliance of God with you.

My earlier arrival on earth gave me the opportunity to teach you some of the ways of this place. I look forward to learning from you the ways of where you now are.

Happy journey, Joddu! May love, blessings, thoughts and prayers accompany you eternally.

Our Shem is one!

Pap

Acknowledgements

I offer my sincerest gratitude to That which gave me strength to walk this path with Jonathan. In your great generosity you offered me your inspiration, strength, valour, thoughts, words, and actions in the most difficult of times. You lifted me up whenever I fell.

Special thanks to all the medical staff who cared for Jonathan, especially Dr. Carol Derno, Dr. Simon Ling, Dr. A Kavadias, Dr. Eberhard, Dr. Gerstle, Dr. May, Dr. Chris Newman and the PACT team – Gurjit, Nora, Rebecca, Carolyn, Lori and Emily – Dr. Berger and his team, and Elena.

I also thank my dear family: Jessica, Blanche, Father Patrick, Ana, Yvette, Proto, Allen, Mark, Allan, Emmanuel, Raymond, Narcissa, Angelo, Patrick, Dr. Prashant, Sonia, Veena, Kalsi, Maria, Archana and her parents, Felix, Barbara and Mugzee. I pray blessings to Jonathan's cousins: Erica, Veronica, Ryan, Shannon, Keane, Charbelle, Raquelle, Michelle, Léo and Thibaut. I want you to know that Jonathan enjoyed your company and loved you all very much. He very much enjoyed the cousins' party you organized for him.

Thank you, too, to the principal, vice-principals, staff and students of Saint Theresa of Lisieux High School, especially to the graduating class of 2014–15 and Ms. Hayhoe. Your thoughtfulness, love and compassion touched Jonathan and is etched onto my Spirit.

I thank Rachel Cooper, who so patiently and kindly read, edited and helped me put this book together, and Harvinder Kalsi for helping with pictures and artwork.

Thank you Shari Morash, Lori Ives-Baine and Coroline Bennett for your guidance and encouragement.

To my son Matthew and my wife, Espy, who along with me experienced Jonathan in a very intimate environment, my deep gratitude for the understanding, love and kindness you emanate throughout our sojourn together, but especially during our difficult time spanning Jonathan's illness, death and the year after.

The creation of this book has been a partnership between Creator, Jonathan, Matthew, Espy and all those mentioned above. Your being there for me extending love, understanding and kindness at a time of intense turmoil and difficulty is what my Spirit travels with and is eternally grateful for.

Thank you. *Dev borem korum.* (May God make it good)

Children's Wish

ALL ABOUT: **Jonathan Anthony Leitao**
(Wish Child Name)

MY FAVOURITES:

Color:	Red/Black	Music:	R&B
Book / Story	The Outsiders	Singer / Group	The Weeknd
Game	Basketball & Soccer	Movie	The Longest Yard
Class / subject	Astronomy	TV show	Modern Family
Toy	Batman	Actor / Actress	Kevin Hart
Food	Steak	Sport / Team	Toronto Raptors
Junk Food	Poutin	Cake	Chocolate Cake
Restaurant	The Melting Pot	Store	
Web site	Youtube	Pet / Animal	Mugzee - my American bulldog

The school I attend is: Saint Theresa of Lisieux CHS– Richmond Hill, Ontario

In my spare time I really like to… Chillax

When I am at home I like to...
Play on the computer
Other:

My Wish is: A media and entertainment center with an awesome chair

I chose this wish because: It is something that I will enjoy together with my family

When I grow up I want to be a: Chef

Sometimes we get donations of tickets to music/sporting events. Would you like to be contacted if this opportunity arises? Yes

Please provide contact email and phone number:

Email: [redacted] Phone No.: [redacted]

Property of The Childrens Wish Foundation of Canada.

Reproduced with permission from Children's Wish Foundation

Contents

Just a kid	1
Baby Santa	11
Shem: the "I" within "I"	17
Exploratory surgery	23
Living water	29
Gandhi's underwear	35
Prayers for Jonathan	41
The nature of love	49
Thought, word, and deed	57
Birth ... death ... eternity	61
Surgery is successful	65
Body and Spirit in pain	69
Prayer as communication	77
Shem: behind the mask	81
"Don't you love him?"	87
Communion with the Divine	95
All is well	101
Snowflake and cherry seed	107
Matthew's support	111
The moment I knew	123
"Jonathan and God have a deal"	129
Accepting God's plan	133
"I don't feel good, Mama"	137
Radiation and a stranger's compassion	141
Do not resuscitate?	147
"There is no need to whisper in secret"	151
"You are going home, Jonathan"	155

Contents (continued)

Parties and laughter	165
Jonathan's awesome couch	173
Saying his goodbyes	175
Jonathan makes a video	179
Guided by Spirit	183
"Am I holding you back?"	187
"I'm done"	195
Counting breaths	199
"What is the taste of this grape that I eat?"	205
Spirits intertwined	207
Suggested Reading	211
Suggested Viewing	212
Other Helpful Resources for Bereaved Parents	212

ONE

JUST A KID

The hospital called," my wife, Espy, said as I walked in the door. "They want us to come in on the twelfth. It was strange ..." Her eyebrows drew together. "They asked if we wanted Jonathan at the meeting as well. Why would they ask that? I told them 'yes' and then they asked me, 'Are you sure?' Isn't that strange?"

I wondered, too. "Yes, but we must go."

It was late morning on the twelfth of May, 2014, when the doctors took us into the consulting room at SickKids, the Hospital for Sick Children in Toronto. After a little small talk about basketball – our son Jonathan's favourite sport – the doctor asked, "Do you want Jonathan in for the conversation?"

"Sure," I said, not knowing what was going to be discussed.

"Are you sure?" the doctor asked.

Red flags went up. We were in the department of oncology, and three doctors and a nurse were in the room. Jonathan was sixteen years old. *He is your baby,* I thought. *He has been through a lot in the last few months. You take the blow. You can tell him later when his health improves. Right now, you take the hit, not him .... He is a kid.*

Out loud I said, "Well, maybe not. Let's talk first and then Jonathan can come back in." I asked Jonathan to let us speak to the medical team first. He was not happy, maybe even a little suspicious. There was no time to think this through. A young man came in and invited Jonathan to take a tour of the facility. *We cannot keep him out for too long, or speak too loudly, or cry,* I thought. *He will suspect something is wrong or hear us.*

"The two of you please sit here, and I will move closer so I can see you both at the same time," the doctor said to Espy and me. "Jonathan has a very rare type of liver cancer."

I was stunned. I can still picture where everyone was sitting and the deep concern on the faces of the medical team. My brain went into overdrive. Liver cancer? How? What? Liver cancer is terminal – does that means Jonathan will die?

"The cancer has spread to most of the liver and possibly other parts of his body," the doctor said.

Oh my God. This could not be happening. I struggled to stay calm. *Don't react,* I thought. *Take in all the information and then decide your course of action.* "So what do we do?"

They explained that the cancer Jonathan had was not treatable and that he had only four to nine months to live. "We could try some chemotherapy, but I don't think that will help."

I knew that cancer, particularly liver cancer, causes severe pain in the final stages. "What about the pain, how do we handle that?" I said.

"Oh, there are a lot of medication choices the palliative care team will recommend. He will probably be dependent on pain medications."

I looked at Espy. No words were exchanged. She looked back at me, shook her head slightly and moved her lips. I will never forget the look in her eyes and what that look said: How can this be? Are they really talking about our Joddu?

"Please, can you give us a moment?" I asked. As the door closed behind them, we broke into a million pieces. Why have we been singled out for this? Why does Jonathan have to suffer? He hasn't done anything. In sixteen years he has already suffered more than most do in a lifetime. He has not even got his driver's license yet. Why? How? Who did this? Who do we turn to? Where did we go wrong? What went wrong? Was he not seen regularly by doctors at two different hospitals? Eight months ago at the specialist consultation the doctors had said, "You are doing very well, Jonathan! We are very happy for you." What happened? *God, what happened!*

"You know, we should not keep Jonathan out of the room for too long. He will suspect something is wrong," I told Espy. So I stepped out and called the medical team back into the room. They told us how sorry they were and that they would do anything to help us through this painful time.

"But isn't there anything that can be done for him?" I asked.

"Unfortunately not. It is a very rare cancer, one that we do not see in patients below the age of thirty."

"We have to bring him into the room. He will be getting anxious."

"Yes," the doctor said, "we have to tell him his diagnosis."

"Absolutely not! We are not going to tell him," I said.

"But we have to," the doctor insisted.

"NO!" I growled back. By my tone of voice and the look on my face, they knew not to argue.

"I can't lie to the patient," the doctor said. "He is a smart boy, he uses the internet. I guarantee you he has researched his symptoms and knows his condition."

"Not our Jonathan," I said. "We are a different family. We care for Jonathan, and he trusts us implicitly. Tell him that we still don't have a conclusive diagnosis."

"I can't lie," the doctor said.

"Okay, then, I'll tell him."

"What if he asks me if he has cancer?" the doctor said.

Not only do we know Jonathan better than anyone else, we believe we are spiritual and that our family is spiritually interwoven with each other. Something told me Jonathan would not ask that question, so I boldly said, "He will not ask. He is my son. If he does, I will interrupt so you don't have to lie. I will say what I have to say."

"He has a right to know – it's his body," the doctor insisted.

"If science is telling us that he is going to die, and there is nothing we can do about it, then what is the point of killing him before he dies by giving him this information?"

The doctor either did not understand what I meant or seemed to doubt my sanity.

"I guarantee you he will not ask," I went on. The doctor backed off reluctantly and sent for Jonathan. He strolled into the room, Toronto Raptors cap askew, a huge smile on his face. They asked him to sit.

"Jonathan," I said, "I am a little upset with the doctors because they still do not have a confirmed diagnosis for you." He looked at me and shrugged. "So we have been discussing what the next steps are going to be for you."

My only thought was to protect Jonathan, that no harm should come to him. Since I believe Spirit is bigger or more important than the body, it made sense to me that if the body was going to be discarded by Spirit, than we – the caregivers – had to look after Spirit that inhabited the body. We had to ensure we did not cause Spirit any suffering. We had to do our best to help and care for Spirit while at the same time helping Spirit discard the body.

"Have you searched the internet to explore your condition, Jonathan?" one of the doctors asked.

Jonathan shook his head. "Nope."

"Do you know what you have?"

"Not really. I'm just a kid," he said. "I just want to be a normal kid and do stuff with my friends."

He did not ask, he did not ask! I knew he would not. I cut the meeting short to give Jonathan no opportunity to ask if he had cancer. The doctor managed to keep Espy and me back for five more minutes.

"This is the first time I have lied to a patient," the doctor said.

"You didn't lie, I did."

As I walked to the elevator and down to the food court, my mind was spinning like a whirlpool.

Liver cancer. Oh my God. Jonathan will die in four to nine months? God, tell me this is a lie. I won't be able to talk to Jonathan anymore? Not see him when I get home from work? The silly things I invented and said to him, like, "Be good, have fun," "Hello, Joddu ... what doing, Joddu?" Who will I say this to? Will he miss hearing this? No. No. No! There are so many people praying for Jonathan, this isn't possible. It is a mistake. Please God, let it be a dream, let this not have happened. We are tired from all the procedures, tests and hospital admissions Jonathan has gone through in the last seven months. Let that fatigue be the cause of this nightmare, and wake us up on the beach in Jamaica – Jonathan's favourite place – to realize the nightmare is over.

Jonathan – jammin' in Jamaica.

The ring of my cell phone brought me out of my thoughts. I was still at the food court in the lobby of SickKids. The oncologist was on the line. "I am so glad you are still in the hospital. I just got a call from my colleague, and I would like to talk to you. Can you please come back up? You can come by yourself – there is no need to bring Jonathan and your wife."

"Okay," I blurted. What was wrong now? Maybe it really was a nightmare; maybe they had realized it was a mistake. I staggered to the elevator and up to the eighth floor, where the oncologist met me.

"I am so sorry to do this to you. We depend on colleagues to provide us a diagnosis, and then ..."

What! What is the doctor trying to tell me?

"Well, I just got a call from a colleague who thinks there is a possibility Jonathan may have stem cell cancer rather than cancer of the bile ducts. Because he is so young and because we do not see bile duct cancer in patients younger than twenty-five to thirty years of age, it is possible this could be stem cell cancer, but it is only a one or two per cent possibility."

"What is the difference?" I asked.

"Stem cell cancer is curable in about six months. I am so sorry to have put you and your family through the past hour and a half, but if there is even a small chance that this isn't cholangiocarcinoma, we should look into it."

"So what do we do?"

"We have to do a biopsy and a laparoscopy in order to confirm whether it is stem cell cancer. We need to take a sample of the liver and lymph nodes, and there is something we see in the right lung that we need to investigate as well. It will be a very lengthy surgery, six to eight hours, and he will have to be admitted for about ten days."

Oh God! Another procedure! Jonathan is so fed up with procedures and hospital stays. How can I get him to agree to another ten-day stay?

"You and your family have to decide if you want to do this procedure," the doctor said. "It is not mandatory, as the chance of this being stem cell cancer is only one or two per cent. I had arranged for the surgery to be done later this week, but once we confirmed it to be liver and bile duct cancer, I cancelled the arrangements. Now I get this information, so I will have to rearrange for the procedure to be done. But, you have to agree first. Do you want me to talk to Espy?"

How can I not agree? If Jonathan has even a point zero zero zero zero zero one per cent chance of a cure, I have to give it to him. How can I not? "No, I will talk to Espy and call you back, but for now please consider that our decision is to do the procedure. Please make the necessary arrangements to do the surgery as soon as possible." I said.

"Because we need to do a procedure on the lung, it will be a very lengthy procedure and will be painful for Jonathan as well. You really should talk to your family first."

"I will talk to them, but consider we are going ahead with the surgery."

"I will wait for you to call before I start arranging," the doctor insisted as I headed for the elevators.

I have to seem strong, I thought. I have to shield him from the distress and pain this information can cause. How can he take this? It is too much for a sixteen-year-old. He is just a kid. He is our kid. I cannot let him feel this pain. I'll take the hit, and he will be okay. We are all praying so fervently for him. Prayers are answered; they do not go to waste. There has to be a benefit from the prayers that we and hundreds of other friends and family are praying multiple times a day.

I got down to the food court, where I had asked Espy and Jonathan to wait. As soon as they saw me, they rushed over with curious and worried eyes. "The doctor is saying there is a possibility this could be a misdiagnosis," I stammered. That's the best I could do. Jonathan was there.

"Really?" Espy said. I knew that tone too well. She was going to erase what she had heard from the doctor and start anew. She was going to hear only the word "misdiagnosis."

Jonathan was silent. He looked at me, and as I looked back into his eyes for a moment, I read, *Misdiagnosis? Really, Paps?* in his typical teenage sarcastic manner.

Three months later, on the seventh of August, 2014, he told me he could recall that moment vividly. It was the first time he'd felt he had cancer, he said. "I somehow felt that something was wrong and that this was the end."

I spoke carefully. "They are not sure, but they think it could be something to do with Joddu's stem cells." I didn't want to use the word cancer; I thought it would be too much. *It will go away, even though they said it is liver cancer and Jonathan has only four to nine months to live. It will go away, whether it is stem cell cancer or cholangiocarcinoma or hepatocellular carcinoma. It will go away.*

So I stood my ground. "The doctor says we need to do another biopsy or something, and that will determine once and for all what this is. Then they will start whatever treatment they need to give."

By this time, and by the tone of my voice, Espy knew that the delight she initially felt might not have been warranted. The drive home was quiet. I held back my emotions as much as I could, but I knew both Espy and Jonathan could read Spirit on my face. I was not my usual self. I was hardly even there. My mind was racing. Four to nine months? His seventeenth birthday is coming up in December. Will he be there? If not, how do we celebrate his birthday?

Though we had not said anything about cancer, I could tell Jonathan was anxious. He was in the front passenger seat, where he'd sat since he became old enough to sit there. "Mama has to take the back seat now," he had proclaimed. "I call this seat from now onwards till I can drive!" How much longer would I be able to see him sitting in this seat?

"Why are you staring at me?" asked Jonathan suddenly. I was taken aback.

"Oh no, Jod, I am just looking out your side of the car," I said defensively. "I'm not staring at you." But, I certainly was.

The procedure was scheduled for the sixteenth of May, only four days away. As our lives unfolded over the next several weeks, Jonathan caught me staring at him often. I could not absorb that this young man would shortly not be here with us, not sitting in the car, not going to school, not playing basketball, not drooling at the sight of a steak. Boy, how he loved steak!

Just a few summers earlier, at a restaurant in Paris, he'd finished his steak, and his mouth was watering as he eyed ours. So I asked him if he wanted more.

"Can I have another one?" he asked, his big bright eyes glimmering with hope.

"Sure," I said.

"Yeahhhhhhh!"

You should have seen the joy in his eyes. The server was surprised and delighted to get him another steak.

"Can I have another, too?" his older brother Matthew asked.

"Sure, encore deux entre côtes pour les enfants," I showed off my fractured French to the boys.

"Sure, Pa, they are probably laughing at you," Jonathan said. The steaks arrived and we all laughed as Jonathan was drooling like a puppy!

"Un peu de vin rouge, s'il vous plaît. Merci."

"An Indian dad speaking French in Paris! It just does not go, Pa," the boys teased me.

"Be quiet, you boogers," I said. We all laughed. Life was good.

TWO

BABY SANTA

When Jonathan was born on a snowy December morning, the nurses gave him a Christmassy red toque and called him "Baby Santa." It was the twenty-third of December, 1997. At 4:00 a.m., in the middle of a blizzard, the baby was clamouring to be born, and the car was sliding all over the road as I drove Espy to the hospital. That early in the morning, the streets were free of traffic, and I drove as fast as I dared. After what seemed an eternity, we reached the hospital.

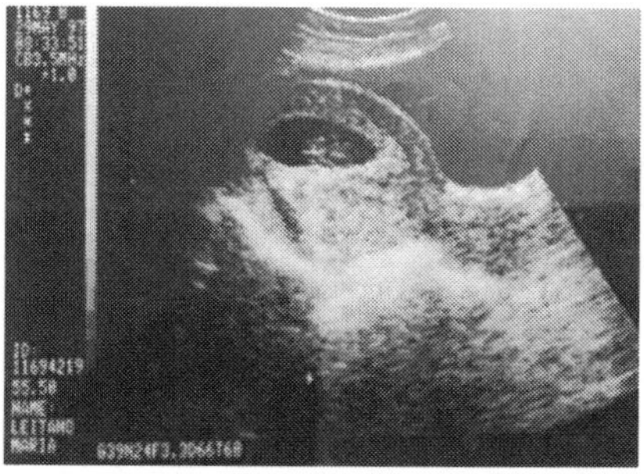

Our first look at baby Leitao.

Jonathan arrived three hours later. "He looks so cute with his hat on," the staff said. "There you go, mum – here is Baby Santa!"

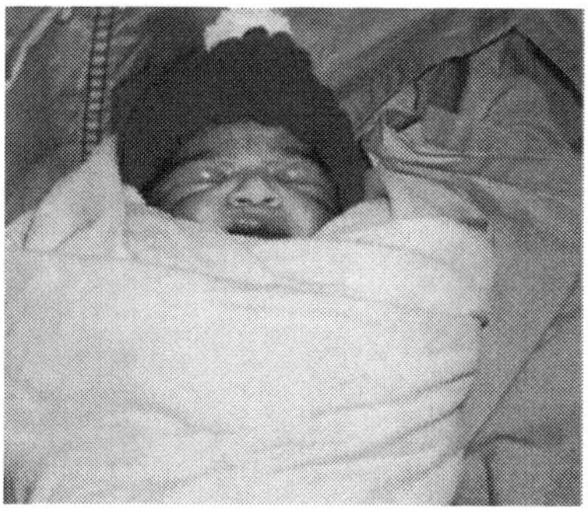

Baby Santa just after he arrived.

We had not decided on a name, so Jonathan came home as "Baby Leitao." What a joyous celebration Christmas it was that year. We kept joking about what we would call this baby, and a month later decided on Jonathan Anthony. The name Jonathan is an adaptation of the Hebrew name Yonatan, which means God given. Anthony was Espy's father's name and since our elder son Matthew had my father's name Joseph as his middle name, we thought Anthony would be appropriate for Jonathan. Matthew was six years old when Jonathan was born.

Jonathan's health made his life difficult from the start. As a baby, he had severe colic and would cry in pain for hours. The only thing that comforted him was the sound of a running tap, so when I got home from work I'd walk around the house for hours with the washroom door open and the tap running at full flow. At three months, Jonathan developed baby eczema that was so severe all his body hair fell off, and he'd squirm with itch all night long. We bathed him almost daily with flaxseed oil; it helped, but only a little. We tried hydrocortisone but worried about its side effects. Then I started researching and found an all-natural cream and ointment, made from the extract of the *Mahonia aquifolium* plant, which we imported from the UK. In a few weeks, the eczema started improving and eventually disappeared. Wow! We continued using the cream instead of hydrocortisone, and as Jonathan grew up the eczema improved so much it was no longer a bother.

Later, Jonathan developed food allergies, and just before his fourth birthday he was diagnosed with ulcerative colitis (UC). After more research, we imported various natural products from the US and Australia. They helped, and around his fourteenth birthday his gastroenterologist, Dr. Carol Derno, was so impressed with the improvement that she asked him if he would speak to her peer group on how he was managing his UC.

"What am I going to speak to the doctors about?" Jonathan said in his typically quiet way. "I am just a kid. I don't know how to talk to them." So we let it go.

Those living with ulcerative colitis sometimes also are diagnosed with primary sclerosing cholangitis (PSC), which is a liver condition that causes bile ducts to harden. At age eight, Jonathan was diagnosed with PSC, and the doctor told us there was a chance PSC could cause cancer in some patients at a later stage. I was devastated. Cancer? What kind of a life was Jonathan going to live? I knew that some UC patients could develop cancer. To know he had PSC was bad enough, but the PSC diagnosis doubled his cancer risk. We were terrified but didn't want to live in fear that he might develop cancer; he might live a very healthy life, too. He wasn't fully healthy, but he could be all right. I researched again ...

From then on, Jonathan ate only organic food. He never ate junk food, never had any alcohol, and ate lots of fruits and vegetables, especially cruciferous vegetables. We did everything that could humanly be done to "avoid" cancer. We visited various shrines and petitioned the good Lord to grant Jonathan good health, and our prayers and petitions seemed to be helping.

When Jonathan was fourteen, his gastroenterologist said he was doing so well that she did not need to see him every six months. Once a year would be fine as long as we kept a watch on the UC.

Two years later, in late September 2013, the liver specialist, Dr. Simon Ling, said, "Jonathan, you are doing so well I feel we should see you once a year from now on. You are growing up nicely, and all your blood work is good. Soon, after your sixteenth birthday, your parents need not come with you. If you want, we can help you kick them out! But after you are eighteen, we will kick you out as well, because you'll have to go to the adult hospital."

It was a good-natured comment from a good, kind and sincere doctor who had looked after Jonathan for the last eight years.

Jonathan had a big grin on his face. "Dr. Ling is so cool," he would often say.

All's well, I thought, Jonathan is healthy. He will do well. Jonathan had just started grade eleven, and we were beginning to talk about what he would do after high school. Jonathan said he'd like to learn cooking.

"That will be cool, Jod," Espy and I both exclaimed. It's good, I thought. Not easy, but good. Even though he's been diagnosed with two conditions, both rare for his age, all that matters is he is doing well.

Over the years, we had great times. We travelled with Jonathan and Matthew to France, Portugal, Spain, Mexico, many Caribbean islands including Curaçao and Jamaica, and we cruised a few times – twice on Disney. We'd observed sea life from the bottom of the Caribbean Sea in a submarine and toured Curaçao twice in a helicopter. We went to Dubai, Abu Dhabi and Oman, where Jonathan had really enjoyed a desert excursion and sand surfing. In France, we dined at the Jules Verne restaurant on the Eiffel Tower.

Jonathan, Espy and me at a Bedouin camp in Oman.

"On the top of the Eiffel Tower?" Jonathan squealed.

"Yes, Joddu, it's going to be something we never forget," I said. And it was! The gruyere-cheese hors d'oeuvres were exquisite and the meal simply out of this world. I vividly recall Jonathan asking for a second helping of hors d'oeuvres. He enjoyed fine food. He could tell if the steak or pasta was not up to the mark, and Italian food made him drool.

Jonathan overcame all his health challenges and grew up to be a kind, patient and delightful young man. He did not speak much, but with his quiet smile he endeared himself to people. He was choosy about friends and had perhaps ten close ones.

That's why, when his school counsellor told me a group of students would attend his funeral on the tenth of September, 2014, I expected to see only ten or fifteen classmates.

It wasn't until Matthew had difficulty holding himself together while giving the eulogy that I looked towards the back of the room.

"We are overwhelmed," Matthew said with tears in his eyes, "with the number of Jonathan's schoolmates who are here. Thank you very much."

Never before had I seen such a crowded room. Not only was there no room to sit, there was none to stand. Students were outside in the hallway. Through the small side door of the hall I could see my work and business associates ranged far down the hallway.

The principal later confirmed to my dear friend Raymond that over three hundred and twenty grade twelve students from Jonathan's school had attended. My God, I thought. I never thought Jonathan would attract so many. He had spoken about a few friends he hung around with, but there must have been over five hundred that attended the funeral that day.

There was so much love and kindness that day that people were thanking us for letting them share in the experience and be a part of the celebration of Jonathan's life. The most frequent comment we heard on that day and for weeks after was that the love and sincerity were palpable in the funeral home and at the church.

Jonathan loved basketball, and until the fall of 2013 the neighbours regularly saw him practising for hours on our driveway. That year he dragged Espy to the Air Canada Centre twice so he could get autographs of his favourite Toronto Raptors. They left early in the morning and stood in line for hours. He did meet his favourite player, DeMar DeRozan, and Jonathan watched every game the Raptors played. When he was in hospital, we watched the games with him, and the staff began to know him as a super supporter of the Raptors. Some of them would come in to watch parts of the game with him.

"So how far will they get this year, Jonathan?" they asked.

"I hope they win," he'd always say, followed by, "but I think they will not go beyond round one."

That's exactly what happened in the 2013–14 season, as the Raptors lost in game seven of round one playoffs. Jonathan took it in his stride. "If they had won, they would have to face Miami in the next round," he said. "I don't think they are strong enough to beat Miami."

Soon I was to see how much more this young man approaching his seventeenth birthday would take in his stride.

His stride lengthened, and what he took in his stride baffled me. And yet, it didn't, because this young man was not just a young man. He is also Spirit – as are we all – which we had welcomed at his human birth and named Jonathan.

THREE

SHEM: THE "I" WITHIN "I"

E*nana urha shrara wa hayye.* These Aramaic words of Yeshua (Jesus) translate as, "The 'I' within 'I' is the way, the truth and the life."

The "I" within "I"? He must be referring to his inner being, the Soul or the Shem. (The Aramaic word *Shem* has a very wide meaning, but in the Bible it is commonly translated as "name.") "Give everything you have to the poor and then come follow me," he said. Is "me" also Enana? In Aramaic, *ena* is the word for "I," and when one says *Enana* it is like saying "I, I" or "I within I." Why did he say "I, I"? Did he stutter, or was it said deliberately? When we read or say, "I am the way, the truth and the life," we have missed an "I"; Yeshua said *Enana*, not *ena*. Could we have misunderstood Yeshua and lost Enana – the real way, truth and life – in our humanness, our senses and intelligence and be deluded to believe that "I" – the human personality – and not the "I" within "I" is the true creation of God?

If we cannot see how wonderful our body is unless we drop our clothing and look, how do we expect to see the wonder of our Divine Soul or Spirit with the human body covering it? But then, can we drop our body, our personality, our ego, our mind, our sense of "I"? Could this dropping be the dying to ourselves that is referred to in the scriptures? If we do this, will we find the "I" within "I," Enana the Soul within the human? When Yeshua called the Pharisees hypocrites, the Aramaic word he used was *apae*, which translates in Latin to *persona* and in English to person. If *apae* is person, are all these the good person, kind person, loving person, generous person, compassionate person, charitable person, church-going person, prayerful person, spiritual person – just beautiful attributes and decorations to a person, to persona, to apae, to hypocrite?

Then who is this hypocrite, this *apae*, this person? And who is Enana?

###

I grew up in Calangute, a quiet Konkan fishing village in Goa, India. My father died when I was six years old, and as our mother had no other means of earning an income, we lived off the land and were grateful for the few gifts relatives and well-wishers gave us. My father's sister, who lived in east Africa, often wrote to my mother and sent us clothing and food items when she could.

One day, a strange-looking, balding man with a mischievous smile walked in our door. Whatever hair he had was long and flowing to the bottom of his neck. He smiled at me, so I smiled back.

"Do you know me, my son?"

"No, sir."

"You are Vincent, you don't know *who I am*?" His eyes turned more mischievous.

My teenage brain went to work. *He knows me ... He expects me to know him ...* A light came on. "Oh! Yeah, yeah, I remember now. Of course I know you, uncle, how are you?" *He has to be an uncle. He is male and old enough to be my uncle. He's got to be my uncle.*

"Ah" said the man with a smile, "I am happy you recognized me." His smile was now impish. "Tell me, what is my name?" ...

Busted! Thank God my mother rescued me, but not before she let my teenage butt burn for a while.

"You don't know *who I am?*" Uncle Xavier had asked me. He could just as easily have said, "I am who I am. You should know me, young man." But he didn't. Instead, he asked, "You don't know who I am?" He knew that eventually I would find out who he was and would gain (through my mother or him) an understanding of who he was. More importantly, although I did not remember seeing him before, there was in him an expectation that I should know him. In those days we did not have phones or Skype; I had seen family photographs, but none of them triggered a recognition of Uncle Xavier.

Uncle Xavier had kind and loving thoughts of his nephew and nieces, and he had sent us gifts when he could. Even though I had sensed a benign, smiling, gentle person, how could I not answer when he asked, "You don't know who I am?" He did not become my uncle from that moment on, he was my uncle from the moment I was born.

It's a pity a town crier had not announced, "Hear ye, hear ye ... here arrives Mr. Xavier D'Souza, husband of Marie Leitao ..." Failing that, a sign saying, "This is your uncle Xavier," would have been helpful. But in the absence of those, I pretended, as I didn't wish to offend him; he seemed like a nice fellow.

I wonder if Moses felt the same way when he tried to entice God to provide a name. "Who shall I say sent me?" he asked. "I have no authority, I cannot speak very well. I am just a shepherd."

"Tell them the Lord your God sent you."

Moses insisted. "If they ask me who you are, what shall I say?"

"I AM WHO I AM."

What kind of an answer is that? I am who I am? Get out of here! When as a teenager I read those words, I stopped reading the Bible, because I felt it was an arrogant statement from God.

Then, after a few years, I started again, because I was too damn curious. Not until my uncle visited me from Africa did I realize that God meant: "You know who I am, man! Why are you asking that question? I am who I was yesterday, who I am today and who I will be tomorrow. Nothing has changed; I give you life, we talked yesterday, we are talking now, I am the same. So I am just who I am."

Just as Uncle Xavier expected me to know him, God expects us to know who God is. God is the reason of our existence. Who is this God? I cannot answer this question for you; we each have to find the answer within ourselves. This is where the Creator God placed that knowledge, and it is still there. Here it was, here it is and here it will always be. It's not in the mountains or in buildings or other places.

To me, God is my creator and I am the creation. Before humans knew the difference between human and other, God existed. Before humans began measuring time, God existed. Before humans were even human, God existed. Conferring human attributes onto God is not right, and yet we do it. By picturing an old man with a white beard bellowing out ten commandments to Moses from the cloud, how are we different from Moses' tribe that created an image of gold and worshipped it?

The problem with humans is that we perceive mostly through our senses. We make statements like "seeing is believing" and refuse to believe what we can't see, hear, touch, smell, or taste. God who is Spirit is not perceivable to our senses. How then can we accept that God is real? Often we feel compelled to project what we recognize through the senses onto God. We say we are created in God's likeness; therefore God must look like us. God existed before humans did; therefore God is very old, and we add a white beard. God is all-powerful, so the voice must be very loud and powerful. In all these ways, we create God in our own image.

Further, we say God is a just God who punishes the wicked, and a jealous God who is angered by those who worship false gods. Really? I believe it is sacrilegious to attribute jealousy to God. Of what can God be jealous?

Jealousy makes humans covet the possessions, education, wealth, looks, fame and other superficial attributes of another person. What do we have that God could possibly covet? God created everything and accumulates nothing. Humans hoard and accumulate wealth, sometimes by stealing from our neighbour, and then say, "God has blessed us."

We are very good at quoting the Bible to justify our self-interest. Not so many years ago, slavery was legitimized by Genesis 9:25–27, in which the "Curse of Ham" was used to rationalize enslaving Africans.

We take a tendency that is all too common in humans, project it onto God and use the Bible to justify this action. God does not want or need to enslave humans; it is we who want to control and enslave each other and maybe even God. Humans are judgmental. If someone does not respond to the prayers in church, we ask why. Is he ashamed of God? If someone sings loudly, is he trying to show off? Does he think he can be a saint by praying loudly? We tell everyone how Jesus is our Lord and say, "Praise the Lord" at the drop of a hat. But what does that prove? Does proclaiming Jesus as Lord and singing his praises make one person holier than another? If we think so, we are as condescending as the Pharisees in Yeshua's time.

Competing for God's attention and expecting a reward in return is to *not* know God.

FOUR

EXPLORATORY SURGERY

We took Jonathan to SickKids as scheduled on the evening of the fifteenth of May. The investigative surgery, to see if this was stem cell cancer rather than bile duct cancer, would take place the next morning.

On admission, Jonathan was briefed on what would happen the next day. They would take samples of his liver, his lymph node and his lung. He was shown the intensive care unit and told he would be recovering there for twenty-four hours and then be moved back to his room after he stabilized.

"No, I do not want to recover here," he said. "I want to go back to my room and be there. I don't like this room."

The doctors and we spoke to him gently. "It is just for twenty-four hours, Jonathan. As soon as you stabilize, we will bring you back to the room."

"No," he insisted. "I don't want to be there, I don't like that room." After the doctors left, Jonathan spoke to me. "Papa, what is this about the lung? Nobody told me about this."

"Jonathan," I whispered gently, "they have found some kind of a lump in the lung that they want to investigate."

"But I need my lung so I can breathe," he said.

Man! This boy is so innocent, I thought. Why, why? But I could not flinch, I had to hold up. I could not let his Spirit break.

"Yes, they are not removing the lung, Jonathan. They are just removing something they see in the lung. They will make an incision and remove it."

"How come you did not tell me about this?"

What do I say now? Do I tell him they want to rule out the possibility that he has terminal cancer? That there is a possibility he has stem cell cancer rather than bile duct cancer? That if it is stem cell cancer he will be well in six months or so? And do I tell him the chances of it being stem cell cancer are only one or two per cent? What will this information do to him and to his Spirit? Will that not make him despair and feel helpless? Will he still want to go through with the procedure?

"Jonathan," I said, "so many procedures have been explained to me in the last few days and months, I am sorry I have missed telling you everything in detail. I did tell you that they are going to do a laparoscopy on your lung."

"I don't know what laparoscopy means," he said. "I don't want to do this now, please let's go home. I don't want to do this."

I talked to Espy, and we both wanted to get Jonathan to agree, even though it would be difficult. How could we not investigate whether he had a hope of being cured? If we didn't do this procedure now, the doctors were likely to get upset at us, and that might have consequences. More importantly, if we did not do the procedure, we had to accept the original diagnosis and wait for him to die. And later, if we found out it was not bile duct cancer and that something could have been done to save him, how would we feel? How could we give up hope? Would that not mean we just lay down and let him die? We might as well have told him he had terminal cancer and there was nothing to do but wait for his death.

How could I do that?

Hope keeps us going. When we go to bed, we hope for tomorrow, though tomorrow's arrival is not guaranteed. We believe there will be a tomorrow and that it will be better than today. Although we may hope that our hearts will beat for a hundred years, we are not guaranteed this; and rarely do we think our hearts may stop beating at this very moment.

Even though death is possible at any time, we are not fully alive if we think only of the possibility of death. Death is inevitable *in* life. Death is *contained* by life, just as birth is. We are born, we grow up, we live a certain way, get sick, heal, age and die. Most life events and experiences are different for different people. But the experiences of birth, aging and death are common to all. If all our experiences were the same, we might as well be ants walking in a straight line, encountering exactly what every other ant in the line encounters. Life is not an event; life is what goes *through* different events like birth, growth, disease, aging, working, playing and death.

When we say "I experienced this event," what is it that these events and occurrences are experienced by? Who is the "I" that experiences these events? When the occurrence of the event is over, how is it that I can re-experience the event even though it is not currently happening? Is the experiencer that which we call Soul, Spirit, Atma, Shem? We'll talk more about this later.

A great teacher told a story of ten bridesmaids and how they should ensure there was sufficient oil in their lamps, so that when the bridegroom arrived, their lamps would be burning brightly. I have heard sermons on this story, about how we the "brides" of Christ should stay vigilant and wait for the bridegroom – Christ – to arrive, and how the bridegroom could come at any time; and when he comes, we should not be asleep or unprepared with no oil in our lamp. If we are unprepared, with no lighted lamp, Christ will be disappointed with us, they said.

I take a different lesson from this story. Having oil in our lamp guarantees only the presence of oil in the lamp. We need to nurture the light in the lamp by keeping it away from an open window on a windy day, or from the veranda when rain is slanting in, or from people who may want to blow out our lamp. We must also make sure the light is not covered and so deprived of oxygen. While nurturing the light with sufficient oil, we must also avoid whatever can snuff it out. To me, this teaching is about doing all we can to nurture our life and ensure it burns brightly while avoiding what can extinguish it. It is about caring for our life – our true and eternal life.

Again Jonathan insisted, "I don't want to do it."

My wandering mind came back to the hospital room. "Jonathan, this is really the last procedure they want to do. After this they will know what course of action to take so you can get better once and for all."

Espy also talked to him and tried to make him understand that we had to do this.

"I am not prepared," he protested. "I thought we were just going to do a biopsy. I don't like this lung thing they want to do."

Reluctantly we told the ward doctor of his hesitation. The staff were gentle and explained that it was to benefit him and that much effort and hard work had gone into arranging the procedure at short notice. Jonathan hesitated and then finally said, "Okay, let's just get it done."

I knew he only agreed because we asked him to, that he would rather be at home playing with his friends or just "hanging," as he'd say. But once he made up his mind to go ahead, he cooperated fully. He did say he felt scared a few times, but when we told him we would be outside waiting for him, and that all of us and especially his Aunt Jess would be praying throughout the surgery, he felt reassured.

"She will pray for eight hours?" he asked with a grin on his face.

"Joddu, you know Aunt Jess, right?" I said, "If she says she will do something, no one can stop her."

He gave me a tender, understanding smile. "I have done all these procedures before, Pap," he said with a shrug. "It is nothing new, really – once they put me to sleep, I won't know anything. It's just this lung thing that I didn't expect. But let's finish it off, and then at least I can go home peacefully. I don't want to go to the ICU, though. I don't like that room."

I told him we should just focus on getting the procedure done and not to worry about the ICU. "We will pray for you to recover well, and you do, too, please."

I prayed all night. *God, please tell me, does he have this terminal cancer they say he does? Is my boy going to die in four to nine months?* I hoped to hear "No," but I heard nothing. Did I have functional ears but not hear and functional eyes but not see?

This was the middle of May. Since the end of February, the doctors' tests and procedures had been to detect signs of cancer. The blood work showed Jonathan's alpha-fetoprotein (AFP) count was increasing. "AFP count is over 25,000, which is extremely high," the oncologist had said earlier that week. "AFP is only produced by the regenerative activity of the liver and by cancer cells. Liver regeneration produces an AFP count of about 500, and Jonathan's count is way above that, between 25,000 and 30,000. Jonathan's diagnosis of PSC about nine years ago put him at a higher risk of developing bile duct cancer later on in life, but, he is only sixteen. We don't see this type of cancer so early in life."

My boy is going to live, I told myself. There is nothing in this world that is going to change that. I have never experienced so many people praying so fervently for one cause at the same time. From Canada, Goa in India, Kenya in Africa, Nîmes in France,

England, Australia and the United States, family, friends, priests and well-wishers were praying fervently for Jonathan's healing. My classmates and priests from Calangute, my home village in Goa, and Father Patrick, my dear cousin-brother, were regularly offering masses along with hundreds of his Jesuit colleagues in Canada, Europe and India. All these prayers would have an effect, I knew.

Goofing around at Mill Pond, Richmond Hill – July 13, 2013.

With cousin Keane at SickKids food court – March 12, 2014.

FIVE

LIVING WATER

When we ask ourselves, "Who am I?" we may reply, "I am so and so, a lawyer, a doctor, the son of a king, a minister, an officer, a postgraduate, a theologian, a scholar, an astronaut, a clerk ..." These establish only our human identity and, one might say, these answers allow the human ego to reinforce and establish itself and in turn Edge God Out (which is what EGO does). Instead of "Who am I?" we should ask a different question. "What am I?" helps to dissipate the ego and assist our true being – the Spirit – to regain its rightful position and re-establish itself as the animator of the human.

What am I? I am an emanation from the very core of the Divine Creator God. I flow from the centre, from the heart of hearts, of the Divine Creator and exist as long as this emanation exists.

Time came later and does not decide the duration of my existence. Time is a humanly created tool for measurement.

I have no name. I was created by Creator, who did not need a name to call me by; Creator is in a continual communion with me. I, the emanation of God, know my Creator through this communion, and this emanation from Creator God is my life. The Creator does not need to call to draw my attention; I am always attentive to the Creator. Without this attentiveness, my connectedness – through communion – to the Creator gets disrupted and susceptible to displacement by the senses. I am a creation of God in the likeness of God. As the Creator God is Spirit, I am Spirit emanating from the Creator's heart and have no home other than the Creator's heart. I exist because the Creator exists. I have no name, no enemy, no predator, no friend, no family, no belonging, no accumulation, nothing. I am Atma, Spirit, Enana: the "I" within "I."

###

As a young boy in Calangute, I often visited a local freshwater spring. Before it became a popular tourist destination, Calangute was a typical Konkan village. Fish, rice and coconut curry were our staples. We would go to school or later to work, return to a nice cup of hot tea with *tizan* or *goddshem* or *alebel'le* or *godache bhakri* – home-made snacks our parents made – and head off to the beach. There we met friends, and we'd sometimes go into the water and sometimes not, sometimes sit on the sand and sometimes not, sometimes walk along the shore and sometimes not.

Sometimes we walked to the hills to eat wild fruit, and there would be cajus and wild berries that we plucked and ate. Later we'd arrive at a little freshwater spring. Cool refreshing water tumbled out of a little opening in the hill. In summer heat when wells ran dry, this lonely spring never stopped flowing pure water. Where did this water, so cool and refreshing despite the heat, come from? No river ran through the hill, and the nearest river was ten kilometres away, but we gave that no thought. We were tired from climbing trees and walking among thorny bushes picking fruits and berries. Our bellies were full, and we were exhausted. Someone had kindly left a small tamyo (a metal pot that could hold about a litre of water) that we used to collect fresh flowing water from the spring and pour it onto our heated heads. *Ahhhhh! This is life!* we'd say every single time.

"I will provide you living water, and if you drink of it, you will not thirst," Yeshua said.

"This is a desert and you have no pot; how will you provide me with water?"

As humans we need a tangible reference point to perceive the Divine. When Yeshua said these words, he addressed them to a human being, someone who was a human (a body) and a being (existence, Spirit, Soul, Atma). In this instance, the human should have stepped back and handed control to Spirit. You see, Yeshua did not offer water, he offered "living water." Water is an identifiable material, but what is living water? There is no such physical thing that the senses can touch. So he was offering something Spiritual. The "human" part of the human being should have stepped back and let the "being" part take control. The "being" is a state of being – in an awareness of the existence of Spirit God and the emanation that is us and God. This awareness is what would have caught Yeshua's words and understood what he said. There would then have been no need to ask the question that was asked, as the Being, Soul, Spirit, Atma or Shem would know – *if* it were given a chance to. This spiritual state of being is an ever-existing *awareness or consciousness* that the human is supposed to perambulate in. When in such an awareness, a human is a *being* in the awareness of its true and real origin.

While walking at night, have you ever turned suddenly and found someone walking a few metres behind you? Or, in a crowded room, have you turned to catch someone staring at you? What made you turn?

This is the awareness or consciousness that surrounds us, or we (human) perambulate in. If we are busy or distracted, our awareness can diminish or disengage, and we miss the spiritual prompt to turn around. When spiritual consciousness or state of being (spiritual net, aura or realm) is disengaged, human consciousness (sight, smell, taste, hearing and touch) takes over. Spirit, in the form of what we know as conscience, may attempt a reengagement, but the human will argue that what Spirit is bringing forth is intangible and therefore immaterial, unreal, impractical, and illogical and so should be rejected. The conscience is Spirit attempting a correction.

Remember when you trained your puppy? You picked it up whenever it looked as though it wanted to pee. Maybe the puppy was too lazy to walk to its designated pee spot or maybe it just forgot, but because you loved the puppy you simply picked it up, perhaps said, "No!" and carried it to its designated pee spot. This correction you give the puppy is similar to the conscience prompting a correction. Eventually when the puppy learns, you joyfully proclaim how happy you are that the puppy is now house trained.

In the same way, when you feel your conscience, it is Spirit prompting a correction. Spirit is telling you that your action is a result of analyzing the wrong data – mostly gained through the senses – and that you need to correct the path you've taken. "Conscience is God's presence in man." ~ Emanuel Swedenborg, (1688–1772).

When Yeshua told the woman at the well about the living water he could give her, her human consciousness, comprising all the human senses and their functions, responded. They were in the desert, standing by what must have been the only source of water for miles, and Yeshua carried nothing with which to draw water. Hearing the words, "I will provide you living water, and if you drink of it, you will not thirst," a human visualizes cool water quenching thirst, just as I did at my village spring. She was at the well in a desert, yearning for water. It is very human to think, *How can this wanderer with no water pot give me any kind of water?*

Yeshua was hoping to engage the woman's spiritual consciousness, and in writing about my village spring, I hope to engage your spiritual consciousness. Perceive God not the way God is portrayed in movies or pictures, but as pure Spirit. No body, no face, no hands, not on a cloud or in a bush, not on the altar or a pedestal. Your Spirit knows this, I assure you.

Do not think, I am so and so, the son of so and so. Think, I am Soul, I am Spirit. I am distinct from the body, from the human. I reside in the human and control the human. The human draws strength from me and without me will wither and die. The human cannot replenish me; I replenish the human. My Creator provides me nourishment and life, I emanate from my Creator like the freshwater spring. God my Emanator is loving, kind, generous and extravagant, setting no limits or restrictions. Supreme and Divine Love emanates from this Divine Being and this is where I come from, this is my home. I am here because I emanate from God. Others also emanate from God: we are all the same Divine emanation. As the moon reflects the light from the sun, so we reflect the emanations of the Creator. Love, kindness, joy, peacefulness, and bliss are some of these emanations. If I tire, I return to the Divine source and am refreshed. I do not have to go to the village spring, I do not have to go to a well and draw water. Divine refreshment is omnipresent; all I have to do is be aware of its presence. Being aware is the ship that carries me to this realm. This awareness or consciousness is the inexhaustible, living water Yeshua offered the woman at the well.

"The kingdom of God is at hand, the kingdom of God is within you," said Yeshua ben Youssef.

If we reflect in this way often, our spiritual consciousness will engage. We will have new eyes that see and new ears that hear. To perceive something in Spirit is not to perceive it with human senses. That is why Yeshua's messages were not accepted. His friends and listeners had eyes but could not see, and ears but could not hear.

Spirit created by God is free, happy, loving, kind, selfless, giving, generous, and lavish. It is the likeness of its Creator God.

SIX

GANDHI'S UNDERWEAR

We all love our children. We do everything we can to protect, love, nurture, and be good to them. When children learn to walk, we know they will fall, so we hold their hands. Some of us even install padded carpeting to cushion their falls. (The guy writing this book thought of doing this!)

But why not install a bed of sharp nails on the floor so our child quickly learns not to fall? "They'll learn the hard way, but they'll learn fast," we could tell our friends.

Those friends might say, "Yeah, you know what? Let's do that at our place, too. These damn kids keep falling down every time we pick them up. We don't fall when we walk, so why do they think it's okay to fall? They're taking advantage – they know we'll pick them up, so they're deliberately falling. Enough of this! A carpet of sharp nails it is!"

We believe in a loving God who protects us, loves us and encourages us to be the same towards our brethren. Yet he sets an ugly monster to scare us, tempt us and take us to hell. Why?

Why would your parents install a carpet of nails when you are learning to walk? The answer is simple: they would do such a thing only if they were inconsiderate, uncompassionate, unforgiving, spiteful, impatient, intolerant, just plain unloving and unworthy of being parents. Now tell me which of these attributes remind you of God? God is the one being who is all good. Therefore, anything God does or creates has to be good. God even looked back at what was created and said, "It is good." God is the sole and Divine Creator, and all that emanates from God is good.

In ancient times, Pharisees and scribes were responsible for preserving scriptures so that the message was not lost, forgotten or changed, and would be taught in the right way for the benefit of others. But these guys also strongly felt the need to preserve their profession. They needed to make a living, and if everyone attained knowledge directly from God, what would happen to these middlemen?

Yeshua said that a light is useless if it is hoarded and preserved – hidden under a bushel basket – but that it should give light to all who want it. The Pharisees and scribes agreed but persuaded us that they were the ones appointed to lead us to this brilliant light, that we could not see it on our own. And so these custodians of Scripture began demanding respect, honour and even worship because they were "specially appointed by God." They called themselves priests of the law. They clothed themselves with expensive and pompous garments, wearing fancy caps of different kinds and colours to indicate their position in a hierarchy they created. To protect and preserve their position, they proclaimed themselves the sole and exclusive distributors (commission agents?) of the word of God. They persuaded us that we were lowly sinners in need of forgiveness and guidance, which only they are appointed to dispense. Common folk brought them food and gifts hoping to earn favour with those in the know and close to God.

And here we are. The process was gradual, of course, happening one piece of misinformation at a time. As the saying goes, little drops of water make the mighty ocean.

They started preaching how bad we the creations of God are, and how by our sins we'd caused Jesus to suffer and die. How we are sinful, unworthy wretches who constantly betray and sin against God. That for this we will go eternally to a fiery hell, where thousands of devils await us with red-hot pitchforks sharpened regularly to stab our butts if we try to sit and get a rest.

An all-loving, forgiving, and compassionate God who creates us in God's own likeness does this to us for all eternity? *Eternity*? When we get mad at our kids, do we stay mad at them for all eternity? Or even for all of our earthly lives? We need to remember that these so-called custodians of the word of God were intent on self-preservation. Without our support, the pedestal they stand on will crumble.

Our human frames of reference can lead us down some strange alleyways. Bapuji Mohandas Gandhi said, "The only devils are those running wild in our minds."

I repeated this to a Christian friend once while speaking fondly of Bapuji. When I realized he was not enjoying the conversation, I stopped, but he took this as an opportunity to counter. "You know," he said to another person who was part of the conversation, "Gandhi was very immoral. He never even wore underwear."

I was nonplussed. "So we judge people's morality by whether they wear underwear or not?" I asked.

"Yes," came the self-righteous reply. "The body is a temple of God. We have to treat it with respect."

"And your friend Jesus wore underwear, did he?"

Dead silence. I could sense his fury boiling up. "God will punish you!" he declared.

Oh man! This statement is used like a weapon to instill fear, and I've heard it so many times that I can now hear it before it is voiced. "Why?" I asked, again knowing what the answer would be.

"Because you have disrespected Him."

"Come on. I just asked if Jesus wore underwear. There is no disrespect here. Did he or did he not wear underwear? I have not researched whether he did or not. You raised the topic, so I ask. According to you, Gandhi did not wear underwear, and that makes him immoral. The same standard should apply to Jesus, don't you think?"

How skillfully we use human standards, customs and traditions to justify our beliefs. Underwear as we know it did not exist in Jesus' time, so he could not even have considered wearing it. But who made the wearing of underwear a morality issue? Certainly not God. And when we are challenged, and the emptiness of our human laws is exposed, we get defensive, angry, and threaten the speaker of truth with the wrath of God, of the devil, and whatever else we can think of that will cause fear, pain and suffering.

The body has pain sensors but Spirit does not, so how can fire burn or hurt Spirit?

Just as we should not project human characteristics onto God, who is Spirit, we should not transfer these same human characteristics onto God's emanating Spirit within us (Enana). We are created in the likeness of God; God is Spirit and so are we. If we accuse our neighbours, does it mean they are actually guilty? Just because we say our neighbour is doing crazy things, worshiping the wrong gods, eating snake meat or drinking blood, does that make our accusations true? And even if they are doing what we accuse them of, can we use our standards, our reference points, to pass judgment and say they are therefore evil and will go to hell? So how does us transferring human characteristics on Spirit make Spirit have these characteristics? Are these not like accusations we make about our neighbour?

Our standards are human constructions, and we cannot set them up as the arbiters for all of God's creation. Some of us believe that God has a white beard and lives in a cloud, but that doesn't make it true. God has no form. God existed, exists, and always will exist as Spirit. And the Spiritual existence of God does not depend on whether we like it or not, whether we make accusations or not, or whether we accept it or not.

> "He sees truly, who sees the Supreme Lord present equally in all." ~ Bhagavad Gita

SEVEN

PRAYERS FOR JONATHAN

We awoke early on the morning of Jonathan's surgery, which was scheduled for 9:00 a.m. He had undergone so many procedures and received anaesthesia so many times in the last few months that he was used to the routine of no solids after midnight. "I can have water, right?" he asked jokingly.

"Of course, Joddu," said Espy in a heartbeat.

For the rest of Jonathan's life on earth, whatever he asked, we responded instantly. "If Jonathan asks, reply three days ago!" I would say.

"I know, Ma," he said with a grin. "I am just teasing you."

Despite the early hour – too early for a teenager to be up – not only was this teenager up, he was in a good mood. This is great! I thought as we prepared and the nurses came in to wheel Jonathan to surgery.

"I can walk there," Jonathan said. "It's no problem."

"But we have this big file to carry," said one of the nurses.

"Can you put it on the wheelchair and we all walk?"

"Sure," the nurse replied.

We all waited outside the operating room. Nurses and anaesthesiologists came by to say hi to Jonathan. Many knew him by now. "He is that tall boy who comes to pick up Gatorade," the lady at the food court recalled once.

Espy was praying. I was praying. We were all praying.

"You ready, Jonathan?" the anaesthesiologist asked.

"Sure."

"Okay, buddy, let's go then."

They wheeled him away to anaesthesia and then to the operating room. As Jonathan waved goodbye and the door closed behind him, Espy and I strained to see him. When he was out of sight, we looked at each other with red eyes, fighting tears.

"He will be okay, Espy," I said.

"I want to say my prayers."

"Okay, I will get some breakfast." At breakfast, I called India to speak with my sister Jessica, who I knew was praying nonstop for Jonathan to be healed.

"I just finished meditating," Jessica said. "I can see him as a young, healthy and strong boy, Vincent. He will be okay."

For a moment I could not speak. "Thank you. God bless you," I managed at last. We chatted for a while, and she told me she was going to pray again, that I was to call her the moment Jonathan recovered from anaesthesia. She would meditate until then, she said.

"But that will be eight hours!" I said, recalling what Jonathan had said the previous night.

"Go now," Jessica said. "Jonathan and Espy need you."

As I headed back to the surgical waiting room, I called my elder sister Blanche and told her that Jonathan was in surgery.

"We went to mass last night and this morning," Blanche said, "and I am going to pray now. Did you get any sleep?"

"Not really."

"Go get some rest while you can. You will be needed after Jonathan wakes up."

Father Patrick, Mark, Raymond and Narcissa, Ana and Allan, Yvette, Emmanuel, Léo and Thibaut – all members of our extended family – had all been informed of the timing of Jonathan's surgery. They and hundreds of others were in prayer. I got back to the waiting room and sent Espy for breakfast.

"I will be in the meditation room across the hallway," I told her. "When you finish breakfast, you can either come back here or go to the meditation room."

As Jonathan's words "meditate for eight hours?" ran through my mind, I thought, *I will do whatever it takes.*

In the meditation room, I sat alone in the stillness.

"This is me and I here," I said into the quiet. "My boy is going to be okay, right? This is a test like Ibrahim's, right? There was no reason for you to want the life of Ibrahim's son. The life of a child does not add to your life, so why would you want a life? Yet you put Ibrahim through a test. Is this my test? Are you testing us?"

No answer.

Tears streaming, I went on. "If so, why does Jonathan have to go through all this? If it is me you are testing, put me in the frying pan – why are you picking on my young son? What has he done? In the Bible there are so many instances where you say, 'Woe unto those who harm the children.' To whom should I say, 'Woe unto' now? Why Jonathan?"

No answer.

I had never cried like that. Slowly, still alone in the meditation room, I began to regain some composure. "You have to pray, you have to meditate," I told myself, taking deep breaths.

"Do not humanize the Divine *Enana urha shrara wa hayye,*" I heard myself say. *Divine Creator knows all. I have to go where the kingdom of God is.* I tried to go within, to be still and meditate, but it was a struggle. Thoughts of Jonathan and what he said to me the previous night kept running through my mind. Images from that snowy December night and morning sixteen years ago were before me. How I had driven Espy to the hospital in Scarborough.

How we had waited in anticipation and through labour pains to finally see this wonderful little boy, his eyes tightly shut. The red toque on his little bald head, how I had bet with Espy he would be born Christmas Day. I lost that bet, but he showed up for Christmas all the same – starting this sojourn on the twenty-third of December, 1997, at 7:40 a.m. Today, I sit here knowing the prognosis for liver cancer and that this is Jonathan's diagnosis.

"The doctors say he has liver cancer," I told Creator. "The prognosis is not good. There is no treatment, chemotherapy or radiation for this. But how can I give up hope? How can anyone give up hope?"

I cannot give up. I will not give up.

Yeshua said, "Ask and you will receive." "If you earthly parents know what is good for your children, how much more does your father in heaven?" "If you have faith, ask that this mountain lift itself and fall into the ocean, and it will be done for you."

Can I ask for this? I can and I do. I ask that Jonathan be well, that God withdraw the cancer cells in him and reverse the cancer. Or that this may be stem cell cancer – that they say is only a two per cent possibility – and that God heal him.

I joined the hundreds of others praying for this innocent boy. God hears the prayers of the innocent and the righteous. Jonathan has prayed asking for healing; he believes he is going to be well. He believes. He is not waiting to see the cure; he believes he is well already. That is why he didn't even want to do this surgery.

There is no cancer in my boy, there is absolutely no reason for a cancer to be in him. He is well. He is free of cancer. Jonathan is recovering. In my mind I see surgeons performing the surgery. *Please, God guide their instruments, minds and intellects that they may do the right things and come upon a way to treat and heal our dear Jonathan. Bless all instruments and equipment and all those in the surgery room. You be there with them, keep Jonathan company, and let him know you are there with him.*

Having worked in health-related fields for more than thirty years, I knew how bad liver cancer was. Being told Jonathan had liver cancer, and the remoteness of the possibility that it was stem cell cancer, never left my mind. This is not going to be easy, I thought. But the Divine can do all, at any time. The Creator is not bound by our rules and diagnosis. Though I was bothered by the multiple procedures Jonathan had undergone over the last few months, that he was so fed up with them, and that his health was not improving, I was convinced our prayers and those of so many others had to have an effect.

Prayers cannot go to waste, they just cannot. Prayers are yearnings of the Soul, of the Spirit, of Atma, of Enana. My Soul emanates from God, so God knows what my prayer is and why I pray. God emanates Love and that means Jonathan, Espy, Matthew, I and all other creations are Love, kindness and compassion emanated by God equally. Our prayers will have an effect – it has to be so.

"Look," I said to God. "Though the doctors are looking to confirm whether Jonathan has liver cancer or stem cell cancer, I believe Jonathan is healed." I thought of the many people who were regularly praying for Jonathan. "Bless all those who are working so hard for Jonathan," I prayed. "To pray is work, too. Just as work produces fruit, so also do prayers. Bless all those praying for Jonathan at this moment, who prayed throughout the past months, and who will continue to pray for him. Bless us and give us strength. It is not easy to go through this. None of us – not Espy, Matthew, Jonathan or I – have trained ourselves to go through this. How could we? We are living it now. Give me strength. Please God give us all strength."

A sharp nagging needle poked at my gut. It would poke at times with the words "liver cancer," and then my faith and belief would neutralize it. This happened too many times not to take notice. *Why is this thought jabbing at me? Jonathan will be okay. This is my belief; this is my faith. So many people are praying for him, and all these prayers will have an effect. They just have to.*

I thought of Angelo, a friend from my village whom I had spoken to earlier that day as well.

"Vincent," Angelo had said, "Nobody knows the will of God. You don't and I don't. Only God does. To ask for healing is right – you have to ask and pray for healing. This is what we are all praying for. But none of us praying, pretending to pray or not praying knows the will of God. The will of God will happen. Accept the will of God first, and then see what it is. Don't insist on your prayer being answered – your wish being granted – and then say, 'God's will be done.' Your wish may not be God's. Do you know what the will of God for Jonathan is? Do you know what is good for Jonathan? For that matter, do you know what is good for you?"

Though his words upset me, I knew Angelo was right. I do not know the will of God, do I? I would have to become one with God and know God's intention to know that. Can I do that in my present condition? I am a mess. The doctors tell me that my boy's life could end in four to nine months. How can I be still and know God and God's will? Yet that is the only way to know God and God's will.

Creator God, I prayed silently, tears rolling down once again. *I cannot do this. This is too much. How can I see my son go through this? He is a child.* The tests and hospital visits started in November last year. Jonathan turned sixteen in December, and we have been in and out of hospital since then. Matthew, Espy and I celebrated the new year 2014 with Jonathan in his hospital room. *God, this is all too much. What is to become of us? Please, please heal Jonathan.*

Angelo's words visited me again like a needle in a feather bed. The prayers and good wishes of so many people strengthened my faith, and I felt sure Jonathan was healed. The comfort from the prayers felt like a feather bed, but then the needle would poke and I'd jump up looking for it. What was it? Why was it bothering me? *God,* I pleaded, *help me understand. What am I missing? What is it you want me to see?*

A prayer flowed through my mind. *Dear God, if this is what is to be, and if Jonathan has liver cancer, please do not make him suffer. He has suffered more than most his age and certainly more than I have. I will be fifty-two in a few days. I know people who are eighty and have not suffered as much as he has. Please consider the pain and suffering he has already endured and accept it as his offering to you. Accept it as you accepted the offerings of the prophets who came before, and save him from more anguish. I don't know Jonathan's path; you and Spirit within Jonathan know that. If his path is to leave this earth and return home, please be merciful and take him from the operating table. Espy will be heartbroken. So will Matthew, so will I, and so will Jonathan's aunts, uncles, cousins and all who are praying for him. But Jonathan will not suffer, and that is the most important thing. If it is your will that he should die, please take him now.*

Fooling around on my 50th birthday.

I wept.

After a few minutes I returned to the waiting room, where Espy was praying. We exchanged a few words. Jonathan was still in surgery. I sat next to Espy and prayed with her. We knew our family and friends were all praying and that masses had been offered. Christian, Hindu, Muslim, Sikh, Jain and Jewish friends were all praying for a miracle.

My sister Jessica called. "He is still in surgery," I told her.

"Call me the minute he wakes up."

Raymond and Narcissa called; they are our best friends and like family. "Jonathan is our son, too," Raymond said. "We are praying very hard for him. All is good. All created by God is good." About ten months earlier, Jonathan had been the ring-bearer at their wedding.

I kept praying, "God, heal him. You can do anything, all is possible, our intelligence does not compare with the Divine, may Jonathan be well."

"I hope this is a bad dream and we wake up soon," Espy said softly.

"Yes, it cannot be true. It has to be a dream," I said, but Jonathan's name was up on the board to say he was still in surgery. *Please, dear God, we want our son to be healed, please hear our prayers. But if it is your will that he is to die, then give us strength to accept your will, and please take him from the operating table. Let it be so. We will be okay. We want Jonathan to be okay. We want Jonathan to be okay ...*

EIGHT

THE NATURE OF LOVE

For the freshwater spring in my village, the hill is not the source. The source is the local water table, which is connected to the other water tables on this earth. The water at the Calangute hill spring is an emanation of this global water table, as are other springs all over this wonderful creation of God. Some flow on a mountain, some flow through rock, and some flow unnoticed into the bottom of the ocean. Similarly, Creator God is the source of all.

Love, too, is an emanation from God. Just as fresh water flows from a spring, Love flows from the heart of the Creator. Not a literal, physical heart, but from God's core, the very centre of God's being and existence.

When Yeshua offered "living water" to the woman at the desert well. He wasn't offering her a bucketful or drumful of material water; rather, he offered her a way to attain the knowledge through which she could refresh her Spirit by knowing and being ever-aware of Spirit (Enana) within herself. This knowledge acts as an everlasting (living) refreshment (water) of Spirit within us. When I say that Love emanates from the heart of the Divine, I mean that like the Divine, Love is a divine, pure, strong, refreshing emanation from the very centre of God. Since God is Spirit, and we emanate from Spirit, we too are Spirit in the likeness of God. Nothing else.

Stay with this feeling. Do not ask: who is this person, who is that one, who is, who is ...? Stop. Just as Love is an emanation of the Divine Creator, so am I. And so are you; therefore we all are composed of Love. As long as the Creator exists, this emanation that I am (Spirit) has to exist. The Creator is eternal, therefore Spirit also is eternal, as is the connection to Creator. We have done nothing to create this; we can do nothing to destroy it. It simply is. "I tell you truly, before Ibrahim existed, I (Enana) am." In order for us (Enana) to die, the Creator would have to die.

What about love being a kind word to my neighbour, a hug to my kids, working hard to care for my family, taking care of my dog, loving my enemy, saying happy anniversary, happy birthday, merry Christmas ...? What about the diamond ring I give or receive at my engagement?

These are all like makeup we put on the Love emanating from God. Light, gentle makeup is okay, but too much of it can make us like a caricature of love! Love is Divine and like the Divine has no shape, form or tangibility to it. The object of my love may feel dissatisfied if I do not take her or him out for dinner, or if I give a gift that does not measure up. It is we who created this need to be reminded that we are loved and then decided that gifts and material things are reminders and signs of love. This is caused by our insecurity, and so we change our behaviour to merit certain gifts and then complain if we think we deserved more: "I was so nice to her, and all she gave me was a cheap pair of socks for Christmas!"

Or a young woman in love may say, "I love him so much. He should have spent at least a thousand dollars on my engagement ring. He just got me a fifty-dollar ring from the grocery store!"

If you are the recipient of a gift, how can you tell if you are "worth" that gift? Have you set a price on yourself, on your work, on your love for the other person? Of course not. And yet we have turned this world into a house of trade where we barter love, kindness and compassion for material things. Rather than be reminded that we are loved, we should know that we are love itself emanated by the source of Love our Creator.

We have done nothing to merit the Love that emanates from the Creator; yet for all eternity, Divine love flows to us. Our donations, sermons, evangelization and similar activities, if done to gain favour with God or anyone else, are exercises in futility. We must do them only if prompted by Divine love within us, the same love that flows from God whether we deserve it or not. "If you do all these great things, but have not love, you are but a gong or a cymbal," said Yeshua.

Our humanness limits our ability to know ourselves and to know God. Human memory can recover only human experience and earthly knowledge; Divine memory can recover Divine experience and knowledge from God and Spirit. The emanation of Love from our Creator flows from the heart of God unconditionally – it envelops us like air. It is always there, we may refuse to use it or deny its existence; for this we receive the consequences.

Then what about all the gifts God gives us? A good family, an education, a good job, a house, a car, gold, diamonds, land, airplanes, friendship with kings and presidents, beautiful hair, blue eyes, brown eyes, dimples ...?

We crave all these material things to make us look good in the eyes of other humans. Once we have them, we want to protect and parade them, hoping to instill in others a sense of awe, admiration and respect for us. Little do we realize that material things are instruments on loan to us in order that we can serve and help other humans to know the true source of all.

We may say, "He has blessed me with all these wonderful things and made me higher than my neighbour." What we mean is, "Look at me, I have done so many good deeds that I have earned God's favour. If you be like me, He will bless you. Let me show you the rules you have to follow."

By convincing ourselves that we can earn God's favour, and in turn God's many, many gifts, we justify to ourselves the piling up of acquisitions. A business associate who owned a financing company adopted the saying, "Greed is good," – and then would soften it by adding, "in moderation, of course."

Yet hasn't greed been the sole cause of war and theft from ancient times to this day? And how would we moderate greed? Is there a greed-governing body that we can appeal to if someone crosses the line?

Greed leads to rivalry, war, acquisition, destruction and callousness. These are not attributes of Divine Spirit, and we are wrong to see material wealth as evidence of God's love. As humans, we know about physical poverty and feel the need to provide for tomorrow, so we hoard our wealth. We overwrite Divine and Spiritual memory with economics, wants, and human logic, and our survival instinct triggers a bloody war. Providing for tomorrow becomes not enough; we need to provide for our children and our children's children. We end up guarding a mountain of material things that we're keeping "for a rainy day." Some charitable organizations and churches have more wealth than they'll ever use, yet their members cannot afford a full meal for their families.

But is it not noble to provide for our families? What kind of parents would we be if we didn't feed our children? God gave us children; are we not right to care for them and provide for them? These are arguments that the human makes to protect and justify what the human has decided is right. And so we accumulate wealth, saying it is for our family.

Throughout our earthly sojourn, we need to be vigilant. Our humanness and our ego – by hook or by crook – are determined to get a foot in the door of our being. Once the foot is in the door, humanness creeps into our heart. And once it's in our heart, we believe only what humanness can validate. Our perception of reality is turned around. Our spirituality turns into "instruction manuals" for the human experience. To discourage others from writing their own manuals, we instill fear of retribution from God and point to the heavens, where superior beings live. We declare ourselves the top of the food chain and say that all other creatures are inferior to us, citing our intelligence as proof. We are a God-fearing nation, the chosen ones, put on earth to be masters of all creation. Since other groups of people are not chosen, we feel entitled to steal their possessions, to violate their women and to starve their children. God punishes the wicked with a mighty hand and makes us victorious, we then say.

But it is all false. We are chosen only by our own selfish human selves.

Like an ever-flowing spring, Love is an ever-flowing emanation of the Divine Creator. In rain or sun, the spring flows, depending not on the rain or the sun, but on the water table deep within the earth. The emanation of Love does not depend on whether we are Christian, Muslim, Hindu, Buddhist, Jain, Jewish, atheist, black, white, brown, yellow, or green for that matter. It does not depend on our caste, colour, creed, religion, or nationality. It depends only on the existence of God. If God exists, all of God's emanations – you, me, love, kindness, joy, peace, etc. – exist. That is it.

After many years or even centuries, a spring that has been flowing can suddenly dry up. Our earth is not as solid and stable as it appears; its core is a moving mass of lava. This is why we experience earthquakes, volcanoes and tsunamis. Sometimes it needs to let out steam, and there is a volcano; sometimes the crust of the earth needs to give the molten core more room to move around, and there is an earthquake or a tsunami. A shift in the tectonic plates of the earth's crust causes the earth to quake; a tectonic shift in the ocean can cause a tsunami. These shifts can affect the water table and cause a spring to run out of water or a river to change course. Archaeologists have confirmed that Egypt's River Nile is no longer on the course it was when the pyramids were built. Think about that. The Nile may have been the crucible of civilization, yet today it is not where it used to be.

Civilizations flourish near water sources. As a community depended on a great river for transportation, growing food, building their houses, bathing and drinking, the older generations would teach the younger to respect it. We should not be surprised that the ancients gave great names to these rivers and likened them to a god. In India, one huge river is the Brahmaputra. *Brahma* in Sanskrit is the name of the supreme God and *putra* means son. So does the Brahmaputra become the physical son of God?

A river's name is given by humans, not by God the Creator. When the Brahmaputra started flowing, even Sanskrit, the mother language of the Indus civilization, did not exist.

Since ancient civilizations were so dependent on water, we can understand how respect for the river would turn into reverence and eventually to worship. The people looked at the river and said, "This is the source of our food and water, this is our God. Let us worship it, make burnt offerings and sacrificial ceremonies so that the river god will be pleased with us and bless us more and more. Let us stop anyone else from tasting this water and refreshing themselves, as God gave this river to us – his chosen people. Those others were not chosen by God. Woe unto those worshipers of trees and animals! Woe unto them."

Little did they realize that, in another part of the world, another civilization similarly flourished. They also had a river that helped irrigate their crops, coconuts, and other fruits. They used the cow to pull their plough and to make yogurt, butter and cheese; and when the cow died they made shoes and clothing from its hide. They may have appreciated the utility of the cow and started saying exactly what the others had said: "This is our God. Let us worship the cow and revere it ..."

We all have the ability to make the same mistakes. Not the tendency, the ability. We also all have the ability to justify our mistakes by saying, "But we meant this and not what you think we meant." We demonize the mistakes of other people by saying they worship the cow, the river, idols, or other material objects. When we humanize the Divine and judge others by our standards, can we not realize our standards are as wrong as we say theirs are? We should not judge, lest we be judged by the same standards. To be a judge, we need to observe as God does. Do we?

Consider this: The Creator creates, looks at the created and says, "It is all good." What does "all" exclude? Nothing. We are the emanation of God, and this emanation is also called Love. Therefore, we are the Love of God, and it is said that God's heart is full of love for us. This love emanates in all directions, and we are all this emanation of Love. We are all the same.

NINE

THOUGHT, WORD, AND DEED

As a young boy I learned catechism. One requirement was to learn what was then called the "Our Father," now known as the Lord's Prayer. Another was the "I confess." In the "I confess" is a statement of admission of sin in "my thoughts, words and deeds" and then one asking forgiveness for sinning. I often wondered, why thoughts? Aren't our thoughts private? They happen in our head and stay there. Nobody needs to know what I think. If I am angry and curse somebody or wish them harm, so long as I do not act upon it, no harm is done. If no harm was done and nobody got hurt, let me indulge in my thoughts – they do not bother anyone. Also, there is no way anyone can tell my thoughts, and if asked I can deny having bad thoughts. How can they prove otherwise? I will think whatever I want; they got nothing on me! God gave me the ability to think, and by telling me I sin by thinking, they are offending God!

Thinking is primordial, innate and essential to being human. If we do not think, we will cease to be human beings. Therefore think we must.

As a child learns to speak, it listens to sound and then tries to articulate the sound it heard. The initial attempts are usually off-target and not correct (off-target = *hattah* in Aramaic; hattah is translated as sin in the Bible), but the child tries again and again until it senses a good response from the people around it. Once a good response is sensed, that sound is repeated until it becomes automatic. Between hearing a sound and articulating it, the child thinks how to produce that sound. It is learning how to use a vocal instrument – the ability to speak. All our abilities and senses are instruments we (Spirit) have been equipped with. Thinking is also one of these instruments, and like the child whose thought precedes production of a sound, our thoughts precede our words and deeds.

The Buddha thought that we should strive to achieve right thought, right words, right actions and right livelihood – and right thought came first. Yeshua went even further: "Anyone who looks at a woman lustfully has already committed adultery with her in his heart." This statement is not about the act of looking or of adultery; it is about the thought at the centre of our being or in Spirit within us. What thought did the sense of sight trigger? Like the child learning to use the vocal instrument, we have to learn to use our instrument of thought generation. Right thought is important to produce right words and actions.

Love promotes the wellbeing of all without expecting anything in return; the ego edges God's love out of our system. We then learn of God through books and scriptures and sermons. We quote chapter and verse of scripture, interpret and argue till the cows come home, go back, and refuse to return. "The spirit will teach you everything," Yeshua said. He did not tell us to write, memorize, dictate, protect or preach the law, but to spiritualize it. When information or impulses received from our senses trigger thoughts, Spirit will teach us and ensure right thought flows. But human brain and intellect interrupts this process with logic, calculation and reasoning and – like a dog being trained to do human-like acts – trains the human to be human-like rather than God-like.

Yeshua spoke from Spirit. He gave Spirit unhindered access and use of his sound and other instruments; his actions flowed from Spirit within and that is why all he thought, said and did was loving, right and kind. We, on the other hand, having let our intellect train and inculcate us, become fixated on doing "great things," and we miss the mark (*hattah* – sin).

I encourage you to think which way of living is from Divine Spirit and which is from the human ego. Once you do, you will regain your forgotten ability to see and hear what God intends. You will see what God wants you to see. In other words, the being of Creator God will be reborn within you and you will know everything.

You are a Spirit Being, not just a human born to make mistakes. You are not the body ... *you are a Soul, a Spirit, Atma or Shem*: that which God the Divine Creator created in the likeness of Divine Creator.

TEN

BIRTH ... DEATH ... ETERNITY

We are trained to believe that we are born into this world courtesy of our parents, that we live, age, and die, and then enter eternal life. But to enter eternal life, we would have to be at some kind of junction awaiting the arrival of eternity. When eternity arrives, we or someone would need to arrange for our bodily death, so our spirit could board the eternity train and live the eternal life in the "embrace of our Creator God." Alternatively, the eternity train could be waiting for us to die and get aboard, or there could be defined events after which a hand-over to eternity could take place. At the appointed time – like a relay baton – we would be relieved of our earthly life and handed over to eternal life. But then is there a similar hand-over at birth? If at death we are handed over eternally to God, then at birth God must have handed us over to our parents. Hold on a second. This means at birth God handed us over, and at death we are returning to God. If God handed us over, then how can we define a time when we (Spirit) were created? We know our body began forming after conception, but when did God create our Spirit?

There is no time when we were created. Our creation – like our Creator – is timeless and eternal. Time is a human concept we have projected onto God. Creator is Creator and we are the creation, we should not project human concepts onto Creator.

"I tell you the truth," Yeshua said. "Unless you turn around (go back to primordial thoughts) and become like little children, you will never enter the kingdom of heaven. Whoever then humbles himself like this little child is the greatest in the kingdom of heaven. And whoever welcomes a child like this in my name (Shem) welcomes me (Enana). But if anyone causes one of these little ones who believe in me (Enana) to sin (*hattah* – miss the mark), it would be better for him to have a huge millstone hung around his neck and to be drowned in the open sea."

Consider these two scenarios. You are at a beachside hotel enjoying the view of the vast ocean. A wind surfer appears on the left, too far away to know who it is, but you feel the enjoyment they are experiencing. You feel the wind blowing on the surfer's face, you can taste the salty ocean spray as the surfer catches a wave and speeds along. Then they glide out of your view. You become grief stricken. "The surfer's life is over," you say, and you begin to weep. Or you are in a city, looking out the window at cars driving by on the highway. Where are all these people going? Can't they take the bus? Suddenly a bright yellow Ferrari enters your view, and you wonder who is driving this car. It must feel great to drive a Ferrari: the power, the comfort, the luxury. "Hey, where did it go? How sad! The driver – God rest his or her soul – only had the pleasure of driving this car for a few minutes. I wonder why they had to die so soon?" You begin to weep.

In either scenario, you could have changed position to see the surfer or the Ferrari again until it went out of view once more. But grief and sorrow overwhelmed you. Your senses brought you no information of their existence, so you are convinced they are dead and pray for their salvation, as nothing else can be done. Meanwhile, oblivious to your conclusions, the surfer continues surfing and the Ferrari driver continues driving. At dinner that evening, you relate the story to your children or friends and say, "I prayed for them, that God may forgive them and accept them in his kingdom (see, I am a good person, I pray for the unfortunate)." We don't know what they are to be forgiven for. Do we love them enough to care? Regardless, we stand in judgment, knowing they need forgiveness.

What humans call time is a window through which we can observe certain portions of eternity. We cannot say when the surfer started surfing and the driver driving, or when they stopped. Only if we see the big picture, showing when they were created and when they cease to exist, can we know. Humans do not see this big picture, but our true self (Spirit) does. Humanization has made Spirit forget. When we regain this memory, we know where we come from, who God is and who we are.

Human intelligence is finite and linear. A is followed by B, and 1 by 2; if there is a high, there must be a low; if there is good, there must be bad; and so on. That is why the woman at the desert well asked Yeshua how he could give her living water and what would he draw it with. She was using human standards. The divine realm, commonly referred to as the kingdom of God, has its own rules and standards not humanly comprehended.

Yeshua's friends asked him, "Tell us what our end will be."

Yeshua replied, "Have you then deciphered the beginning that you ask about the end? For where the beginning is, there shall be the end. Blessed is the man who reaches the beginning; he will know the end, and will not taste death!" Gospel of Thomas – saying 18.

When did the surfer start surfing and the driver driving? When God willed it. When did God will it? That is not our question to ask. That is God's prerogative.

Yeshua told a story about how we should not take the best seat at the table in case a more important person is invited. The host would then have to ask us to vacate the seat for the more important person. "Rather, take the lowest seat, so that when your host calls out to you and asks you to sit next to him, you will be honoured," he said. The host is Creator; Creator will assign us a seat at the banquet, not the other way round.

Yeshua, why did you not explain this story more clearly? Why did you speak in parables and expect us to draw out the real meaning?

The eternal emanator of Love observes whether we take a position that is not rightfully ours. If need be, we will be corrected and shown our place. But if our communion with God has been drowned out by our human intellect, righteous talk, rules, protocols, traditions and customs, then we will insist on sitting in the best chair, proclaiming our greatness and how the banquet has been prepared exclusively for us by God, and how others have been denied a place at the table.

Through this pomp – this clash of cymbals and gongs – how can we hear or feel a loving and gentle nudge from God?

ELEVEN

SURGERY IS SUCCESSFUL

Six-and-a-half hours after Jonathan was taken into surgery, the surgeon came out.

"The surgery went very well, and Jonathan is recovering from anaesthesia."

Thank you, God, thank you. He is going to be okay. The surgery is over and he is recovering.

I was delighted. I called my sister Jessica right away. Even though the hour was late in India, I knew she would be awake, and I wanted her to get some rest. "He is recovering, the surgery is over, and the doctor said it went very well," I told her.

"Thank God! I will get some sleep now, okay?"

I called other family and friends – Blanche, Patrick, Raymond, Angelo, Proto, Ana and Yvette – and told them all the same thing. While I was finishing the calls, the nurse called to us to say we could now see Jonathan.

"He said he is in a lot of pain," the nurse said, "so we gave him a shot of morphine. He should feel better soon."

"Joddu," Espy called out, "we are here, okay?"

Jonathan shook his head and whispered, "Lot of pain," as tears rolled from his eyes. Espy and I both rushed to wipe the tears; then I held back to let her do it.

"Too much pain, Mama," Jonathan cried. "Do something, Mama, please." The nurse gave him another dose of morphine. As only one parent at a time was allowed in the recovery room, they asked me to leave.

"We will get him to the ICU shortly – you can wait there," she said.

Instead, I went to the meditation room for a few minutes. *Thank you,* I prayed. *He is going to be okay. The surgeon told us they had planned for an eight-hour procedure, but things went well and they were able to finish in six-and-a-half hours. That is fantastic! It will be great to go somewhere this summer with Matthew and Jonathan and put the last few months behind us. Thank you, God.*

I walked into our hospital room to take some things into the ICU and looked up in surprise. An orderly was wheeling Jonathan's bed into the room.

"Is he not supposed to spend twenty-four hours under observation in the ICU?" I asked.

The nurse's response made me grateful to God: "The doctor said there is no need for that," she said. "They feel he performed very well in surgery. They have observed him recover and feel he doesn't need to be in the ICU."

Thank you, God! Thank you. This is a miracle. I am so grateful. Jonathan did not want to go to the ICU. He will be so happy.

I whispered to Jonathan what the nurse had said, and despite his pain he smiled his appreciation. There was a line set up for antibiotics and another for morphine, and he was given a button he could press periodically to give himself a booster morphine shot.

"The pain is too much, Papa," he whispered. His eyes told me how much pain he was in. What could I do, how could I take his pain away? I racked my brain for something, anything to relieve

Jonathan's pain. As he healed he would feel better, but I had to help him now. "Should I take a booster?" Jonathan asked.

"Yes, yes, of course take it," I urged him.

"I don't want to get addicted to this morphine, Pa."

"Joddu, you will not get addicted – don't worry. You have to stop the pain now. As you heal, the pain will reduce and the morphine will be stopped."

"Are you sure?"

"Yes, yes – please, Joddu, take the booster."

That was how we managed Jonathan's pain. He constantly wanted not to take the morphine booster, and we constantly reassured him so he would take it.

Matthew came to see him, as did Raymond, Narcissa, Ana, Proto, Blanche and Mark. That night was difficult. We were all tired. By now, most people in the hospital knew that both Jonathan's parents were staying with him. In some wards they allowed it, and in some they didn't but looked the other way. The surgical ward did not allow it, so we were not given an extra mattress as we had been in the other wards.

Matthew teaching Jonathan to climb a tree.

"How will you manage?" Espy asked me.

"You don't worry, Espy, I'll find a way."

As it turned out, I would not need a mattress that night. Jonathan needed help and attention. I could see the anguish in his eyes; I could feel his pain.

"I am not sleepy," I said to Espy. "I'll watch over him, and when I feel sleepy I'll wake you up."

Turning to Jonathan, I told him I would sit in the chair next to him while Mama rested and then I would take a break. He felt this was a good plan and did his best to settle in and get rest, but neither of us slept that night. Pain, discomfort, pain, tubes, noise, pain ...

"Try to sleep, Joddu," I whispered.

"I can't, Papa. I want to, but I can't."

Strangely I was neither sleepy nor tired. Through the night I prayed or helped Jonathan move the bed sheet or shift a tube to a more comfortable position or simply held his hand.

"You will get better, Joddu," I told him over and over. And I knew he would. God did not take him home while in surgery. God could have but did not. The surgeon had said he did better than expected during surgery, and he had done well enough not to require twenty-four-hour observation in the ICU. *This is all good, he is well, thank you, dear God.* Although I did what I could to make Jonathan comfortable, he was perturbed, anxious and troubled, like disturbed sediment at the bottom of a lake, and multiple whirlpools spinning at once.

The surgery took place on the sixteenth of May. Tough as that day was, the next day, a Saturday, was even tougher.

TWELVE

BODY AND SPIRIT IN PAIN

Jonathan had not slept a wink, even with the sleeping aid they gave him. As a result, he became almost delirious, suspicious and scared of everything. The surgeons had requested an x-ray of the lung that had undergone surgery.

"I am scared," he said again and again. As I had the previous day, I looked into his big sparkling eyes – eyes that I loved – and experienced his Spirit in pain. As I write now, it seems strange to write, "I experienced his Spirit in pain," but I can't express it any other way. It felt strange and foreign. Was I delirious too?

I had not slept all night but felt super alert. I observed everything relating to Jonathan while other things passed by; I neither noticed them nor cared. But anything to do with Jonathan got etched into my awareness. His pain I could see was beyond his body. It was in his Spirit, his Soul, his Enana, and he was suffering. *I cannot take this, God. I cannot see him like this – please help him. Ease his anxiety, soothe him, stop this deliriousness and let him sleep,* I prayed. *I cannot bear to see his Spirit perturbed like this. The body will heal and so will his Spirit, but right now, his Spirit is in unbearable pain and needs immediate care.*

I looked up as a nurse came in. "We need to get an x-ray of your lung, Jonathan. Do you think you can walk?" I glared at her in angry disbelief. Jonathan glanced at me before shaking his head. He knew I'd make sure he wouldn't have to walk if he didn't want to. When the nurse did not insist, I relaxed and gave Jonathan a smile and a wink, and his look told me he got it. Espy came along as they wheeled the bed to x-ray, as did the young day nurse who had looked after Jonathan the previous day. She seemed new at her job (I'm not sure) but was kind and compassionate. I was thankful she was with us.

They needed an x-ray of Jonathan's right lung from where they had removed a lump. This part of the surgery took the most time, as they had to make an incision into the lung, and this incision was causing most of Jonathan's pain now. The surgery and incision were necessary, so Jonathan's pain was no one's fault. He had to go through it, and we had to watch, pray and hope for healing and relief from this pain. It hurt within me – not in my body, but in my Spirit. I could feel Jonathan's pain very clearly in my heart, my core ... my very being. *Please God, help him. Ease and relieve his pain. He will heal, we know he will heal, but ease the pain now, please.*

Every time Jonathan took a breath it hurt, so he was taking as shallow breaths as possible. Yet he needed to breathe deeply to expand the lung, because if it collapsed that would be a disaster. Every time he coughed it hurt, yet he had to force coughs so the lung would expand. It was difficult to look Jonathan in the eye. When I looked, I experienced his despair ... his Spirit in pain. *How has it come to this? How can this much pain be heaped upon such a young boy? And I can do nothing to help him? I have to see this? It is not just seeing. I feel it, too.* I could not actually feel his pain, yet I could. *Is this what it's like when Spirits are connected to each other? Is this what being in Spirit is like? Is this what it means to feel another's pain? This is not human; this is wholly Spiritual.* The pain was too much, yet I would not look away. How could I? If I did, would I not be the priest in the story of the Good Samaritan who crossed over and walked by on the other side of the road when he saw a wounded and dying traveller? I will be beside my son doing everything I can. I will look right into him and not turn away.

"Honey, we need to get a couple of pictures of your lung, okay?" the x-ray technician said. "Only one parent can be with you. Who do you want?" I volunteered, as Jonathan would need me to lift and support him, so Espy waited outside and prayed that all would go well. She, too, knew Jonathan was in pain, and she knew he would need my help. So I went into the x-ray room with Jonathan. He cried out as they moved him onto his side to get a chest picture.

"T-t-too m-much pain, Papa," he gasped, tears rolling down his cheeks. He was taking morphine boosters as often as he could, yet the pain did not relent. The technician needed to position him for the x-ray, and this movement spiked the pain.

"I just need to take a few breaths to calm me down, just five breaths," he pleaded.

"Okay honey, I will count to three: one ... two ..." The technician continued with her work.

"I ... I can't do this, please, please, I can't do this!"

"We need one main picture, than that's it." As they positioned him for the picture, Jonathan screamed in pain, the scream causing even more pain as the lung expanded.

"I can't ... I can't!!" Jonathan looked into my eyes in anguish. *God, I cannot bear to see this. How can this be right? But I can't look away, I have to look at him when he looks at me.*

We were both relieved to hear that the picture was taken.

"We just need to ensure it is okay."

Jonathan was trying to catch his breath and collect himself. He seemed to be counting his breaths, something I had never seen him do before. It was not that he was counting, but he was breathing rhythmically, as if centring himself in yoga.

"We need to redo the picture."

I was horrorstricken.

"You moved when you screamed, Jonathan, so we have to redo the last picture. Just the last one and we're done, okay?"

Tears raced down his cheeks. He dared not cry because crying hurt, he dared not shout because shouting hurt, he dared not scream in pain because that hurt, too.

"P-please, can I have a minute with my dad?"

"Let's just finish this picture, then you can talk to dad all you want. Okay, honey?" Why do they use "honey" and other such tender words when they don't mean them?

The nurse who accompanied us interrupted. "He needs a break," she said softly.

"There are other patients waiting, too," the technician replied firmly.

So they moved him. Jonathan was spent. He could not even use his hand to support himself, and he slumped onto his right side – the side of the surgery. In absolute agony he looked at me. I will never forget this moment. "Please help me," he whispered. I reached out to grab him, but where was I to hold without hurting him? Incisions were on his back and the right side. Tubes and other gadgets were attached to the other side. As I leaned forward and hugged him with great care, Jonathan put his hands around my neck and lifted himself up. I grabbed his right hand, and somehow he managed to straighten himself up. This relieved him a bit. I have not and do not want to forget the *look* of that *sound, "Please help me."* It is as vivid now as the day it happened. As I write this nearly one year later, I have to stop, because I can hardly see through my tears.

"Okay, honey, let's get you to – ."

"Stop it!" I snarled. "He needs to compose himself. He needs five seconds – five seconds, he said! – not a count of three!"

"I have others waiting," she shot back.

"So get them in, we'll wait!"

Everything went silent. I'm sure the technician and the young nurse heard the roar of the ocean emanating in that silence – it was my thoughts. "Look at him!" I said. "Look at him. Can't you see his Spirit is in anguish?"

Both of them eyed me as if I were either insane or not from this planet. *Why did I use the word "Spirit"?* And yet I was thinking, *How can they not see it? It is so obvious ... it is so damn obvious. If his jugular were ruptured and blood were flowing, alarm bells would go off, calls would go to the emergency department, and doctors would rush to stop the bleeding. After it was over, everyone would sigh with relief and say, "You gave us a scare, Jonathan, but you are okay now, thank God. Let's finish this little thing we need to do, okay?"*

But here was Jonathan, his Spirit spent and bleeding.

"I just need a few breaths to calm me down, just five breaths," he had said.

"I ... I can't do this, please, please, I can't do this!" he had cried.

"P-please, can I have a minute with my dad?" he had pleaded.

How could a health care worker not see it? I wondered how the wounded traveller had felt when the priest crossed to the other side of the road and walked away without even looking at him. Where has the "care" in "health care" gone? Why do we now call ourselves part of the health industry and not health care providers? We can only care if we love.

I heard the technician whisper, likening me to a body part far away from where my words had popped out. They could call me whatever they wished. I'd achieved my goal: Jonathan needed a break, to breathe and compose himself, and maybe in that time his Spirit would be a bit more at peace. My heated exchange with the technician distracted her enough that Jonathan got the breather he needed. He grabbed onto both my shoulders and moved himself into a position that the technician found to be perfect. We waited anxiously for the verdict on the x-ray image.

"Oh, it's perfect, Jonathan, excellent job!"

Jonathan cried again, but this time it was in joy. He and I looked into each other for a moment. Those big bright eyes, so beautiful when he laughed, were filled with pain. Morphine was helping but only somewhat. He was afraid and in pain, and his Spirit was broken. *What can I do to make him better – please, what can I do?* I thought of God as I asked Jonathan, "What can I do to help you, Joddu?"

His reply hit me hard. "Just be *here*, Pap."

"I am here, Joddu, what else can I do?"

"Just be here. We'll figure out the rest. We're a team, right?"

"Yes, Joddu, we are a team. I'll be here, you be sure I'll be here." That little statement seemed to make him better; I saw that it did. It was not the statement so much as the intention – the thought – that gave rise to this statement that touched and assured him. This thought travelled in the form of words from my Spirit to his, from Enana to Enana, Spirit to Spirit, Shem to Shem.

The assurance "I am here" made him feel better. It did not matter what Jonathan's need would be, nor did it matter if I could satisfy that need. Just the assurance and my presence made him better. The important thing was being here in body and Spirit. In Yeshua's story, the Samaritan was the only one present in body and Spirit. He "felt for" the wounded man. The first passerby (a priest) was present neither in body nor in Spirit. The second passerby felt pity but did nothing. By acting solely out of loving concern for a stranger, and ignoring plans that he might have made, the Samaritan was God-like rather than human-like. "The kingdom of God is at hand," Yeshua said. Jonathan did not ask me to "be there," or be on call. He asked me to "be here," to be at hand.

Similarly the kingdom of God is here, ever-available to us, not there, waiting for us to come to it; for the kingdom of God is within us. As Jonathan did not have to call or "reach out to" me, so also we do not have to call or reach out for the kingdom of God. It is here.

As Jonathan was being wheeled out of the x-ray room, Espy greeted him warmly, asking how he was. Once she was reassured that he was as well as he could be, she turned to me. What I expected her to say was, "You should not have shouted at them." But she surprised me with, "Good thing you told them off – they need to know how to care for someone in need. They don't understand!"

"You heard?" This was an x-ray room with radiation-blocking doors and walls.

"I could not understand what was actually said, but I heard you say something and felt everything go quiet. I knew immediately why you did it, and I am so glad you did."

"It just happened," I told her. "I had not planned on saying those words, but they just came out of me as if pushed through my sound system by another being."

"Thank God that is over," she said. "Now we must pray that Jonathan can pee soon."

After major surgery, the bladder sometimes loses memory and doesn't function as it should. Jonathan had not passed any urine throughout the night, and the nurses were becoming anxious.

"It is important that he pee," the kind young nurse said. She suggested a few tips, including turning on the tap, because the sound of running water can help. "I don't really want to catheterize him," she said gently, "but if he doesn't pee in a few hours, we'll have to."

Jonathan began to get anxious again, and so did Espy and I. I called my sisters in Burlington and India, then I called Angelo,

Raymond, Narcissa, and Dr. Prashant – a friend in Mumbai who is a healer. Espy called her family, too. We asked for fervent prayers that all functions of Jonathan's bladder be restored and that he be able to urinate naturally. Espy and I prayed too.

"Please God," I heard Jonathan pray, "Please, I have never asked you for anything. Now I ask you this small and simple favour. I have peed many times in my life. It really is not a difficult thing to do. But now it has become difficult for me. Please God, help me pee." He prayed this simple innocent prayer many times. We assured him that God would hear his prayer.

"God always hears the prayers of children, Joddu," Espy told him. But as it got closer to the time the nurse had set, it was obvious they would have to catheterize him.

"Mama!" Jonathan cried, "God is not listening to me!"

THIRTEEN

PRAYER AS COMMUNICATION

The Mahabharata is one of the two major Sanskrit epics of ancient India, and in it the sage Kripacharya is an important character. *Kripa* means grace, favour, compassion, tenderness, lovingkindness and Love; *acharya* means preceptor, and teacher or guide (or both). Kripacharya tells his student, "When corruption enters rule or life, milk is made to appear red in colour, the meaning of words is made to change, and loyalty is demanded to the king – *not* to truth and justice."

Our loyalty is to be only to God our Creator, not to the creation or the king or to anything the creation has created, appointed or deputed. Law, books, culture, tradition, habits and the like are human creations. Creator is the sole Creator, existing since before the person (persona, *apae* or *sharira* [body in Sanskrit]) began writing words and compiling books. Everything emanates from God, so love, scripture, law and intention also emanate from God and existed when God thought or intended them and not when the creation began sounding, writing or proclaiming them. The human should claim no credit for voicing, writing or compiling what God emanated. Yeshua did not insist on rules; he actually broke many and – to his eventual physical detriment – encouraged his friends to break them as well. He did not go to the temple on the Sabbath, and he defended his friends when they were criticized for picking corn from the fields on the Sabbath to satisfy their hunger. Rules are created by the human in order to keep fellow humans in check and, sometimes, so that the custodians of the law, the judge and the accuser can maintain their holier-than-thou attitudes.

"The meaning of words is made to change," Kripacharya told his students. When we look at the big picture, the meaning of prayer has been changed by society, religion and the law. Prayer is made to be a set of words that have three or four parts: typically, asking for forgiveness, praising, asking for stuff, and thanking. But prayer is neither a defined set of words nor a plea for material goods, gifts of health and prosperity, and our enemies to be brought to justice. These are corruptions of prayer. Often, the moment someone says, "Let us pray," we prepare to utter a preassembled set of words whose meaning we may not even know. As children, we are given "official" prayer books, and if we can't recite certain of the books' prayers, we are disqualified from receiving some sacraments. We may have been told to read only approved books on religion and that reading unapproved books or prayers could lead us astray. We may have been taught to recite a particular prayer at a birth, at a meal, in the morning, at night, and at a death. And we may have been told that a particular prayer was written by a high priest or a saint or Yeshua himself, and so it is more powerful than our own prayer.

But isn't prayer a communication with God our Creator?

The next time I meet a friend for coffee, should I first pick up a set of words from the dictionary or online and read them aloud to my friend as we sip the fresh coffee? Or maybe I should memorize these words beforehand, so I won't seem to be reading from a script. Should I also expect my friend to have similarly prepared a set of words for our visit? Imagine the conversation:

I: Good morning. How are you?

Friend: Good morning. What did you think of the game?

I: The coffee is really fresh and good, eh?

Friend: Yeah, they played well last night.

I: I hope the prices don't go up again. We can't afford too much coffee at these prices.

Friend: That was a bad penalty call, don't you think?

I: Maybe I should switch to tea.

How often do we communicate *at* instead of *with* others? From a distance, you might conclude that my coffee friend and I had a cultured, respectful and meaningful conversation. Yet, when we parted, both of us would be thinking, "What was that? I don't think I'll have coffee with him again." Communication is first engaging Spirit and then – only if needed – using the human instruments to speak, hear, touch, smell and maybe even taste so that the human intelligence realizes that this communication is tangible and real. Engagement of Spirit, however, is primordial.

FOURTEEN

SHEM: BEHIND THE MASK

Several ancient languages have words that are similar to the Aramaic word *Shem*, whose meanings include Spirit or true self. In my mother tongue of Konkani, for example, someone could say, *Tujea paichea navan haum tukam ullo martam*. An elder person, a teacher or someone who deserves my respect could use it to make me stop and pay attention to their words. It's a gentle version of "Pay attention!" Its sentiment comes from heart, Soul, Spirit. If an elder passerby saw me eating mangoes from my neighbour's tree, he would gently tell me not to do that. If I did not change my ways, he would then say, *Tujea paichea navan haum tukam ullo martam; heam tum kortai tem bonnkor*. The literal English translation is, "In your father's name I beckon you; stop this that you are doing." All this person needs to say is, "Stop what you are doing." So why does he say, "In your father's name I beckon you"? Does he know my father?

Whether or not he knows my father doesn't matter. He is letting me know that in the absence of a teacher, mentor or *kripacharya* – at that moment – he is assuming these roles that would have been performed by a father. He is elder and deserves my respect, although whether I recognize this and give him the respect he deserves is a different issue. I *should* respect and pay attention to him. He does not need to know my father or even my father's name, but he has to fully know the true father aspect existing within (his) Spirit. The authority to make this statement is given to him by father aspect of Spirit, that True Spirit – *tat sat Atma* – within himself. The elder does not think, *Why should I tell this child to stop? He is not eating my mangoes, he is not my child.* Rather, he thinks, *Spirit in this child is an emanation of God, the same God that emanates me. I am Spirit (Atma), this child is also Spirit. Just as I (human) have to continually remember I am Spirit, the child has also to remember. As I learn to remind myself of my Spirit nature, I help others remember this Divine Truth that sets us all free.*

I may choose not to accept his kind offering; this action is mine to perform and depends on whether Spirit in me has manifested a student/child aspect of Spirit within me. When our human intellect is firmly engaged and in control, we forget Spirit and push it into a corner thereby missing gentle spiritual nudges and guidances. So that I will know where the mentoring is coming from, he uses the words, "In your father's name I beckon you." Only if the elder is unable to fully embody *father aspect* will he need to use his body to either hit me or call the authorities. This is not how Divine Creator intends us to relate with each other.

This *father aspect* is the intending thought that gives birth to *kripacharya* in the elder and child/student in me. It is the same Father aspect of Spirit in both, manifesting two different thought patterns, one of *kripacharya* and the other of child/student. Because Gandhi gave rise to the freedom movement in India, we call him the "father" of the nation, but he did not actually cause the nation to be born. Similarly, this Spirit that gives rise to *kripacharya*, child and student is our father. Father is the causative intention that manifests likeness, love, understanding and knowledge in Spirit within all of us.

How can we ensure love is included in the things we do? Can we measure love and add a scoop of it to our actions? Should we be giving our children valentine hearts every time we read them a story or help blow their noses? And how many hearts do we allot for each loving act? Try as we might, we cannot measure the intangible. Just as we are emanations from God, so love, peace, kindness, empathy, compassion, generosity, understanding and oneness with all are emanations flowing from Creator to our Spirit and in turn reflect from the centre of our being (heart) to the heart of the objects of our love.

In almost all English-language versions of the Bible, the Aramaic word Shem is translated as "name." Although "name" is included in Shem, that is not its entire meaning. When we bring home a puppy, we give it a name; it has no original name. And just as the puppy learns to respond to the sound of the name we give it, we learn to respond to ours. But our name identifies only our human person or body, not Spirit.

Behind the mask of our persona is absolute truth, that which Yeshua referred to as Enana, the "I" within "I" – Soul, Spirit, Atma, or Shem. This is the real and eternal me and you that emanates from God. In Aramaic, Shem refers to that which is behind the mask, that which is bigger and greater than the body, the true essence of the person. Shem encompasses everything that animates the human person and is eternal. When we meet someone and comment, "What a wonderful spirit he is," or "She lifted everyone's spirits," we are perceiving the person's Shem.

Shem is your true self, the "child of God" created in God's likeness. It is pure, innocent, kind, loving, gentle, compassionate, selfless, trusting and self-giving. The Creator God caused the existence or gave rise to this "child"; all thoughts, words and actions of this child are caused by the Creator. In the New Testament, Yeshua's friends complained to him, saying, "Someone is working miracles and casting out demons in your name. We tried to stop him because he was not following us." And Yeshua replied, "Do not stop him, because no one who does a miracle in my name will be able soon afterwards to say anything bad about me. For whoever is not against us is for us."

Now let's restore the original Aramaic words for "name" and "me": "Someone is working miracles and casting out demons in your *Shem*. We tried to stop him because he was not following us." And Yeshua replied, "Do not stop him, because no one who does a miracle in my *Shem* will be able soon afterwards to say anything bad about *Enana* ..." Enana is the "I" within "I." Please ponder, what is it that is within "I" or within me? Isn't it Shem? That which is behind the mask, persona or person?

God clothed Shem with a human body so that Shem, Spirit, Atma could have a human experience, not the other way around. This human instrument is easily misled by its human senses and untrusting of Spirit created by God and residing within this human instrument. "Be aware of sheep in wolves' clothing," Yeshua warned. But too often we choose to heed the warnings of "leaders and influencers" instead. We look for spiritual experiences in the Himalayas, temples, churches and at retreats, when what we seek is within us.

If we accept this truth, we will know who we are and what it is to have eyes to see and ears to hear. If we let all human information flow to Spirit, then Spirit's response will be not only childlike but Godlike. No need for analysis, advice, double checking with scholars, professors or anybody else. When the human instrument is prevented from interfering in God's process and from interrupting it, we can truly tap into the source of all knowledge emanating from God. This is our sustenance. Then we – like the spring in my village – will have connected ourselves to the true source of all knowledge, to the living water that is always new and ever flowing.

In gratitude, Yeshua exclaimed, "O Father, Lord of heaven and earth, thank you for hiding these things from those who think themselves wise and clever, and for revealing them to the childlike." The father he addressed is Shem – which gives rise to the childlike in all of us.

FIFTEEN

"DON'T YOU LOVE HIM?"

Mama, God is not listening to me."

Espy looked at me, and we were both thinking the same thing: What can we do? What should we try? How do we help Jonathan?

The nurse walked in. "Any luck?" she asked gently.

"He is trying," replied Espy.

"Okay," she said, giving us more time. We could not wait much longer to catheterize, so I started preparing Jonathan the best I could. He was getting anxious and more confused as I gently explained the process to him.

"How long will they keep it in?" he asked.

"I don't know for sure, but a day or two, then the bladder will get back its memory and you will be able to pee again."

"What kind of a God is this?" he asked me and Espy. "He did not listen to my prayer. Why won't he listen to my prayer?"

How could we answer? Espy had tears in her eyes; I had fire in mine. Seeing Espy's tears, Jonathan controlled himself. Espy helped him to the washroom once again, turning on the tap and handing him cups of cool water as the nurse had suggested.

By myself in the hospital room, I wanted to grab God with my left hand and put a bloody gun to his head with the right. *You listen to prayers, right? You always answer the prayers of children, right? We are to pray unceasingly, right? Right! Show me the answer! Show me! Why are you quiet? You can't answer? Did you not boom out to Moses from that damn cloud and supposedly give him those commandments? Did you not call out to Ibrahim and tell him to stop killing his son? Did you not call out to Suleman and tell him something?*

At this point, I didn't care to recall what God had called out to Suleman about. Why should I care what this God told Suleman, Job, Noah, Tom, Dick or Harry! Still no reply. *You won't answer, eh? Do you know what is in my right hand? Do you want to say hello to my li'l friend?* Al Pacino would have been delighted at the way I said that!

I phoned Jessica.

"What happened, Vincent?" We both shed tears as I told her. "While praying, the story of Abraham came to me," she said. "Just like it was for Abraham, this must be a trial for you. Don't worry, all will be good in the end."

"What trial? Who is the criminal on trial here? Who is it that needs to put me or Jonathan on trial, to torture Jonathan? This is the torture of an innocent child who has done nothing to merit it. And if this Abraham is so great, why have you changed his name?"

"What do you mean?"

"I mean that his real name is Ibrahim, not bloody Abraham." I was becoming agitated. "If his story is so great, why did they change the name?"

"Stop this, okay? We all need to focus on Joddu. You debate this when Joddu is better."

I needed that. It helped me back off a bit.

The look on Espy's and Jonathan's faces said it all as they came out of the washroom. Jonathan would have to submit to catheterization. Needless to say, he was disappointed and disillusioned. He did not say a word, but I wouldn't have blamed him if he'd said he hated God and that God could go to hell. Those were my sentiments, too.

We called the nurse and gave her the news. She was sad, too, but this needed to be done; delaying catheterization could rupture his bladder. When the nurses came in, I leaned over and gently hugged Jonathan while also blocking his view of the procedure being done. He was in tears. I did my best to soothe him, and despite the IV and other apparatus attached to him, Jonathan did his best to return my hug. The nurses were excellent, and the catheterization was done sooner than we all expected. The ordeal was over. Jonathan asked a few questions, and cautiously he started tolerating, accepting and letting go.

I was still wide awake. "Why don't you take a nap?" I said to Espy.

"I took a few naps – you have not slept at all since yesterday."

"I know, but look at me, Espy, I am not sleepy or tired. Take a nap. I will sleep later, and you stay awake then."

The nurse walked in to ask how Jonathan was. "I know movement is painful, Jonathan," she said gently. "You do not have to move till tomorrow, so try to get some rest. The respiratory therapist will come by and help you exercise the lung. You need to expand the lung – we cannot let it collapse. You are doing very well so far, Jonathan. Keep up the good work." She turned to leave. "Exercise the lung, okay?"

Jonathan nodded. After the nurse left, he asked me, "What will they want me to do now?"

"I am not too sure, Joddu, but I think they are referring to some breathing exercises to expand the lung. The lung is like a balloon. During yesterday's procedure, they made an incision in it, so it is kind of punctured. We have to ensure it is made to work so it does not collapse."

Matthew's arrival lightened the atmosphere. Matthew is like a curious cat: he sees levers and buttons on the bed and has to know what they do. On an earlier occasion in another ward, Matthew pushed a button that made the bed rise all the way. Jonathan was laughing from almost five feet above the floor. When Matthew was little, he was mischief personified and often got into accidents. A neighbour with a daughter a few years younger jokingly called him Bandage Boy in honour of the bandages he sported here or there nearly every day.

I was sure he would do something crazy to lighten the mood, but Matthew saw that Jonathan was suffering, so he simply sat by the bed and talked to him. They have a unique, almost strange, way of talking. To me it's as if they're speaking in partial sentences, but they understand each other without needing to finish sentences or even words.

Despite a six-year age difference, Jonathan and Matthew got along well.

This time was not much different, and some things were – I am sure – said to make fun of Espy and me. That lightened the atmosphere and made Jonathan happy, and being happy soothes the mind, calms Spirit and promotes healing.

Matthew insisted that Espy and I take a break. "Go for a walk," he told me. "How long has it been since you exercised?"

"Oh, I'll be okay, don't worry about it."

"At least walk outside while I am here with Joddu." On his insistence, I went to the meditation room while Espy took a nap.

Jonathan, do you know me?

Boy! I really lost it at this God guy. How can God be threatened with a gun? I imagined God easing out of my left hand and entering the gun and animating it. What then? I could be staring down the barrel of my own gun!

The question in my mind was still not answered, though. God did not answer the prayer that came from Espy, me, and many others; and moreover from an innocent sixteen-year-old who is diagnosed with terminal liver cancer. This boy not only prayed, he pleaded.

Why must he plead? Don't you love him? You claim he is your child, but do you see me wanting to torture Jonathan? How come you want him tortured? You feel no compassion? Maybe you should not be in this God business. Why don't you retire like the last pope and let someone younger do what you can't do? I'll take over. Give me the power to heal and do all these great things I should "be able to do if I believe." I would immediately heal Jonathan, and all this anguish would end. Not for just Jonathan and us, but I'd end anguish for all. Then all would be happy, just the way you intended us to be. Go ahead – retire! You can't hear, you can't see, you can't feel compassion. You are a crippled and disabled God. Why did you not answer Jonathan's prayer? The Bible is full of stories where God has "heard the prayers of the faithful and saved them from their afflictions." Was Jonathan unfaithful? Are Espy and I horrendous wretches? I need to know. How else can I correct the horrendous wretchedness that is causing you to torture not just Espy or me but our innocent sixteen-year-old son?

As I walked back into the hospital room, I heard giggling. Matthew was helping Jonathan do his lung exercises. Thank God and thank Matthew, his spirits were good. We had a bite to eat, and very late that night, as Jonathan finally fell asleep, Matthew left for home.

"Wow! Excellent!" I said to Espy. "Now let him sleep. It's good for him."

I rolled out the sleeping bag Matthew had brought and lay down. Thirty-six hours had passed since I had woken up, and I was still not tired or sleepy. Again I prayed. *God, I need to know what this is I am going through. Some friends tell me this is a punishment from you, that I am not following the real and true God and am pursuing false gods. Some have quoted from the Bible, "For the sins you commit, God punishes your children and your children's children." Another said, "Do not say 'Om' – this is devilish. You can't even tolerate touching a hot cooking pan – the moment you touch it, you pull back your hand. How will you tolerate the fire of hell, Vince? It is an eternal fire, it never ends. Say the name Jesus. It is a very powerful name, say Jesus. Because you speak against the church, God is sending hardships your way."*

Did Yohan the Baptist not speak out and tell Herod to correct his ways? Did Yeshua not tell the Pharisees they were wrong, and did he not tell his friends they needed to correct the way they pray and think of God? If he taught his friends to change their thoughts, words and actions does it not imply their existing thoughts, words and actions were faulty? If Yeshua had not brought this to their attention, how would his friends know they'd gone astray and accept a correction? If Gandhi had kept silent, would I and all from India have become free of an oppressive conqueror? And what would have happened if Martin Luther King had not spoken up? "Yet, see what happened to each and every one of those guys," a learned friend told me once.

So then what am I to do, dear God? Let this injustice, hypocrisy, double standard, egoism, spiritual slavery, and corruption just play before me? Do I simply watch those in power misinterpret your teachings, instilling fear, guilt and unworthiness in your children while they enrich themselves? Aren't we all your children? Then why should some enrich themselves on the bent backs of many?

How can I believe that you, God, the loving and only Creator, will take my young son hostage? We call terrorist and hostage takers cowards. Should I not then call you the same? By saying that you will punish my children and my children's children for my sins, have you not set an example for all to be hostage takers? And who should negotiate with a hostage taker? Is this how you control my actions, by threatening and instilling fear in me? How is this any different from us using you as a threat – "Don't do this, don't do that, God will punish you and send you to burn in hell." Are you a beating stick with which we are to correct and ensure good behaviour? Then why did you inspire Yeshua to say, "If you do the greatest of things but have not love, you are but a cymbal or gong?" Come on, it's just you and me here. If you deny that, I will tell you Yeshua also said, "I do nothing of my own initiative, but I speak just what the father taught me." Heh, heh, busted!

Love is the main ingredient here. You know it, I know it, Yeshua knew it, Yohan the Baptist knew it, Bapu Gandhiji knew it and all the great saints, sages and enlightened teachers knew it. Love is the core, the centre, the very heart of you. You are true and unchanging for all eternity. Your Love is emanated onto me, and I reflect that Love as the moon reflects the sun. The moon can do nothing else – it does not generate light. So also I reflect your qualities and can do nothing else – I do not generate any qualities. My thoughts, words and actions do not affect you; rather, they should reflect you as the moon does the sun. My calling you a coward or anything else is casting a human characteristic on you. Humanizing God is pasha, a Hebrew word meaning to transgress, violate, revolt against authority or confusing the creation with Creator.

In the midst of these thoughts, I fell asleep.

SIXTEEN

COMMUNION WITH THE DIVINE

Sometimes I wonder why Yeshua's friends asked him to teach them to pray. Did they not know how? When we come to understand what prayer is, we feel the need to relearn how to pray. We are taught to pray by uttering words, but if our prayer lacks love, then the words are only so much noise. However, we cannot add love to our prayers, and the only way prayer can contain love is if love itself is the source of prayer. God, as the source of everything, is the source of prayer. Spirit within us reflects the prayer, and this Divine communicative reflection from God to Spirit and back to God is called communion.

"Communion" is a word the ancient Greeks assigned to a true and comradely partnership, friendship, fellowship or marriage. It represented a Divine relationship, a relationship with Spirit and not considered human. A human cannot cause or break a communion; a human can only turn away and pretend the communion does not exist. As humans, we breathe without noticing our breaths, but if we stop breathing, we die. In the same way, whether we are aware or not, Spirit is always in communion with Creator God, and if this communion stops, our Spirit is as good as dead.

Spirit, communes comfortably with God. "God is Spirit, and the people who worship God must worship in Spirit and Truth," Yeshua said.

The woman he was speaking to replied, "I know that Messiah is coming. Whenever he comes, he will tell us everything."

Yeshua replied, "I (Enana), the one speaking to you, am he."

To the Pharisees, Yeshua said, "I am the good shepherd. I know my own and my own know me. Just as the father knows me, I know the father, and I lay down my life for the sheep."

Could he have meant, "Enana is the good shepherd, ena knows ena and ena knows ena. Just as Creator Spirit knows Enana, Enana knows Creator Spirit, Enana lays down life for the sheep?" This would imply Creator Spirit "blueprints" or gives rise to experiences (a plan) the human (sheep) should follow.

In ancient traditions too, there were prepared sets of words that people of those times used as prayers. Yet Yeshua's friends asked him to teach them to pray; from listening to him, they realized they needed to rethink the way they prayed. They must have felt an emptiness very much as my friend and I did after our coffee conversation. They must have realized prayer is communion – a relationship not human but Divine – rather than empty human sounds arranged in a perpetual supplication mode. When we are in perpetual supplication, we say our morning prayers, travel the day, and say our nighttime prayers in supplication. How then is our Spirit throughout this day if not supplication itself? What are we doing to this emanation of God all day long? We have prayed and been very religious, some may say, but really have we not been pressuring our Spirit into supplication and therefore changing the nature of our Spirit – God's creation in the likeness of God? Have we tried to remodel Spirit?

We have to be able not only to answer that question sincerely, but to act on it. Remodelling our Spirit by changing its character is like recreating our Spirit. There is only one Creator; we are not the Creator, we are the creation, and our actions must reflect that. This by no means makes us worthless. Creator has a purpose for emanating us, and the knowledge of this purpose is continually emanated to Spirit, who sets the way in which the human is to be operated. When this communion is pure and unadulterated by human interference, the human is like a child and lives according to the prompts of Spirit. The human may try to dominate Spirit, to forget the existence of Spirit, to make rules for Spirit to follow, and to place layer upon layer of human behaviour on Spirit. But by subjecting the emanation from our Creator to humanization and exchanging the mask with that which wears the mask, we counterfeit the creation of God.

Spirit's direct communion with God undoes this counterfeiting and makes the human realize it has to let Spirit do what it knows to do. Spirit knows how to pray; human has to learn from Spirit. Human teaching another human is like the blind leading the blind. In communion with Creator, the human joyfully takes a back seat, becomes still and lets Spirit lead.

Asking for material things creates an expectation to receive. "Seek first the kingdom and all the rest will be added onto you."

Where is the kingdom so I may seek it?

"It is within you and it is at hand," Yeshua explained to his friends. They wanted his help to understand and strengthen the communion between God and Spirit, which the human tries to dominate. They asked Yeshua to help them liberate Spirit, because those who worship God worship in Spirit and in Truth, for the father seeks such worshippers. Maybe they now understood the words, "My sheep hear my voice, and I know them and they follow me."

If we look again at the story of the elder trying to stop me from eating my neighbour's mangoes, we see that this can happen in peace only if the elder knows the father aspect in Shem and I know the child aspect in Shem. Both of us must respond in Shem or Spirit; a human response from either of us will provoke a confrontation. If we are in Shem, we recognize and relate to Shem in others, and those in the same Shem are one another's brothers and sisters. So when Yeshua told his friends to pray in his name (Shem), he taught and urged them to be in a "state of being" (Shem) similar to his.

As humans, we supplicate, plead and sacrifice so as to be "favoured" with the choicest blessings from God. But just as the rain falls on all, God does not choose. God created all, blesses all, favours all and loves all. By saying that a certain race, creed, cult, or group of people are the chosen people of God, we humanize the Divine and justify being part of that group. Our true justification, however, is that we are emanating from God.

When one is continually aware of a communion with God, one's Shem is like that of Yeshua, so praying in Yeshua's Shem is not praying by uttering the word Yeshua, or Jesus – that is a sound we use to refer to the human body he used for his earthly sojourn. Yeshua's Shem is all his Spiritual aspects and awarenesses, and we are to pray in this Spiritual aspect and awareness. We are to be aware that we are Spirit and God is Spirit. Only then are we true, the communion true, and the prayer true.

This is Divine Shem, Spirit, Atma and essence. God seeks this Shem and knows it; we the creation in turn look for it. When we perceive and see it, we realize it is what gave rise or birth to us, it is our Creator and deserving of our respect, loyalty, love and obedience. We therefore accept all corrections given to us by Shem the Creator, because we know and joyfully accept that it has authority over us.

Prayer – communion – elevates Spirit within us to be in harmony with God. By giving human a correction, it makes our Spirit like that of God, so that we can worship in truth and in spirit as the Creator is Truth and Spirit. In this state of being, there is no want, no need, no craving – all is provided.

"In my father's house a banquet is prepared for me; my father knows my every need, my every want. I shall want no more." Prayer gives the human an understanding of Divine Will and then makes us receptive to the will of God.

SEVENTEEN

ALL IS WELL

It was Sunday morning.

The young, kind nurse walked in to check on Jonathan. The nurses had not bothered him through the night, and whatever they needed to do was silent and on tiptoe. He had rested well; Espy and I had also got some rest.

"We need to get another x-ray done today, just to see how the lung is doing."

My Spirit dropped, and so did Jonathan's. The nurse, noticing, hastened to reassure us. "Oh, it will not be so bad this time, I promise – just one picture."

They wheeled the bed to x-ray; no one dared ask him to walk this time. In the x-ray room, the technician was guarded, and just in case, I had my snarl on.

"It is just the main picture of the chest, Jonathan. The one we take of the full front of your chest. That's it."

I was getting ready to do battle, and Jonathan saw that. "It's okay, Papa," he whispered. "We'll be okay. I think I can do this. Just help me move my feet off the bed, and watch these tubes and wires, especially the catheter." I did as he instructed.

"We are ready to take the picture and will come and position you, is that all right?" the technician said as she walked up to Jonathan. Jonathan held onto me cautiously, stood up and positioned himself against the x-ray machine before she could reach him.

"Wow!" all of us exclaimed at the same time. She just had to move him slightly. I stood and supported him, and the picture was done in no time.

"Way to go, Joddu!" I exclaimed.

"I prepared myself," he said. Later, he explained to me how he had played out the scenario of the x-ray clinic in his mind, that he had used yesterday's experience as reference and visualized where they wanted his chest to be. Based on this, he had played out what he needed to do and practised it in his mind. Wow! I thought. Who taught him this?

Back at his room, the doctors were waiting to follow up on Jonathan's progress. The surgeon came and talked to us.

"He is doing really, really well for such a major surgery," he said. "My only concern at the moment is the slight fever recorded by the night nurse. I want to watch it for today; hopefully it does not come back. But as far as the surgery and healing go, he is doing really, really well."

Excellent! I thought. Jonathan is doing well. Excellent!

Then the doctor from the department of oncology showed up and so did my snarl. Fortunately, Espy was helping Jonathan in the washroom, so I got a chance to meet this doctor outside the room and explain that we had not informed Jonathan of his diagnosis and would decide on letting him know later. I told him not to mention oncology, cancer or any similar word or statement within Jonathan's hearing.

"Of course, of course," the doctor agreed. "We know you have chosen this way, so I am going to be very cautious. I am just here to see his progress and how he is doing." I was pleased. He finished his work and said some encouraging words to Jonathan before going on his way.

Jonathan had noticed me glaring at the doctor. "Papa needs to relax," he told Espy. "He is being rude to the doctors."

I explained to Espy that we needed to ensure the environment around Jonathan was conducive to healing. If we break a bone, no medicine or doctor heals it; the body does the healing. When we get a bruise, creams and ointments are only to keep infection away, not to heal. Healing is a divine ability conferred on us by God. Medicines, doctors and everything else are here to ensure a clean, pure and healthy environment. God through Spirit within prompts the healing of the body.

A sower went out to sow his seed. And as he sowed, some fell along the path and was trampled on, and the wild birds devoured it. Other seed fell on rock, and when it came up, it withered because it had no moisture. Other seed fell among the thorns, and they grew up with it and choked it. But other seed fell on good soil and grew, and it produced a hundred times as much grain. The one who has ears to hear had better listen. It is not just the seed, but the environment that is important as well.

The next day was my fifty-second birthday. As soon as Jonathan woke up, he got off the bed to give me a gentle hug. "Happy birthday, Pap," he said. This was the second-last time he hugged me; the last time was in the second half of August.

My sister and her family, Espy's brother, sister and her family, my cousin Father Patrick, and friends Raymond and Narcissa visited us that evening. They brought us home-cooked food and sang Happy Birthday, wishing it were in better circumstances. But to me the circumstances didn't matter. I was where I was to be: with Jonathan, doing all I could to serve, help, and maintain an environment of love, compassion, understanding, kindness, peace and patience. Such an environment is Divine and created by God to facilitate healing of Soul, Spirit and body.

Jonathan showed a big improvement the following day. He was speaking well, and they were able to start weaning him off the IV morphine. The fever left, and the doctors began considering discharging him. Word of this speedy recovery spread, and staff from other departments came by to see this young man who was recovering so fast.

Wow! I thought. *We are experiencing a miracle here. Thank you, God. Thank you. Our boy is going to be well.* I felt strong, my faith felt even stronger, and we kept praying. I called and told those praying that Jonathan was doing so well that even the doctors were pleasantly surprised at his recovery. Everyone thanked God for his recovery. "He is going to be well. Thank God." I said.

Usually, Jonathan would want to go home from the hospital as soon as possible. He would ask us to inquire of the doctors when he would be discharged. He was tired of being in hospital so many times and for so long. This time, however, I was the one anxious to get him home. I knew Jonathan was more comfortable at home, as were we all.

"When can we go home?" I asked, even though they had told us this admission would be between ten and twelve days if all went well. Now it was just five days.

To my surprise, I heard, "Well maybe in a day or two."

I was delighted. "Joddu," I said excitedly, "we could be going home tomorrow."

"That will be great, but aren't you being over-optimistic, Papa? He said a day or two, not tomorrow!"

The next day brought even more improvement in Jonathan. I went to the meditation room and meditated in gratitude, thanking God for healing Jonathan and for the strength we were all gaining. Through Jessica I sent messages to Angelo, to the healer Patrick San Francesco, and to Dr. Prashant and others. Patrick, Angelo and I are from the same village in Goa. However, I know Patrick only through Angelo. Angelo was getting Patrick to do healing sessions for Jonathan almost daily. All were delighted and grateful that Jonathan was doing well. What a wonderful thing!

All is well, all is well, and our ordeal is over. We have to continue our focus on Jonathan, help him recover and regain his strength. To our delight, that afternoon they confirmed that Jonathan would be discharged. I called home and told everyone the good news. "Jonathan is improved so well, they are discharging him today, after just six days. They expected it to be ten to twelve days. This is excellent, he is healed so well – thank God."

Jonathan, however, was not so excited. "There are so many things to be done, Mama," he said. "All these tablets, the morphine, the antibiotics, the nutrition, I don't feel comfortable." To our shock, he added, "I think we should stay another day."

Previously, when the doctors told him he would be discharged, he celebrated. This time he delayed, even asking the nurses to hold off removing the IV. "I want to be sure," he said. The paperwork was done. He was discharged but still hesitant. "Can I stay another day?" he asked the nurse.

"I am sure we can arrange that, Jonathan," she replied. "But why? You are well. The surgeon who operated on you has confirmed that you can go, and he will see you in a few days anyway. Also, we would have to move you to another room, as this one is assigned to another incoming patient." Hesitantly, Jonathan agreed to leave the hospital that evening.

Did he know this was to be the last time he would stay in the hospital? Did he want time to say goodbye?

Allan, Jonathan's uncle, met us at the main entrance of SickKids Hospital. We were going home!

Jonathan is well, he is healed; all is well. Everything will be well. For the next few weeks, Jonathan continued his improvement. My confidence returned. I went back to work, and not a cell in my body doubted his healing. The words of Yeshua came to mind:

"Whatever you pray and ask for, believe you have already received it and it is done for you." I made this my affirmation. Yes, I believed Jonathan was completely healed; I had absolutely no doubt. *I am very grateful, dear God. Thank you!*

EIGHTEEN

SNOWFLAKE AND CHERRY SEED

About a week after Jonathan's discharge, we followed up with his operating surgeon. I drove Jonathan to SickKids, and while he was in the washroom I had a chance to speak to the surgeon privately. "Please do not mention anything about liver cancer," I said. "We have not spoken to him about that." My belief remained that Spirit is larger and more real than the body and that if science is telling us Jonathan's body is afflicted with a terminal illness, we should ensure Spirit in Jonathan is not in torment. A holistic caring for Spirit as well as body is what health care should be, regardless of the outcome. Similarly, whether we are granted a miracle or not, we should commune with God. Communion is what makes the human aware of the existence of Spirit and the nature of God's plan.

"Not a problem," the surgeon said. "I just need to see his surgical incisions and ensure they are healing, that's all. The oncologist will look after the other part." I was glad to hear him say this. He directed Jonathan to the examination table and expressed surprise at his wound healing. "Whatever you are doing, keep doing it, Jonathan. It's working very well. The scar can take up to twenty-four months to fully heal, but the wound is healing really well. Good for you, young chap!"

Jonathan's face lit up like the sun and his bright eyes twinkled like the evening star on a clear night. "Let's go home!" he said.

"Do you want anything for old times' sake?" I asked.

"Nope, let's just go home." He took control of the radio in the car as usual, and off we went.

As a snowflake needs to acquire more flakes, moisture, and cohesion to become a snowball, so a single embryonic human cell develops into the heart, lungs, brain, bones, teeth, and more. How does this cell know to do this? Neither the parents nor anyone else on earth instructs it to develop in such a way. Yet this tiny, microscopic cell develops into a full human. Could God be teaching through Spirit emanation? Could God also be providing corrections if needed? Who else can create an environment conducive to the evolution of human body parts, organs and senses?

Many seeds appear similar, but in the right environment they emanate plants and trees that are like their parents. All this potential is in the seed, yet our human senses cannot tell by looking at the seed what fruit it will bear. If the human does not see, does this mean the seed will develop into a tree that produces rabbits instead of fruit? If we know God has a plan and that this is the best plan for us, why do we ask God for this or that? Do we think God doesn't know? Or do we think God forgot to pack this or that into us when he created, as we may forget our passport in the rush to catch a flight? The seed is fully provided for. The cherry seed does not compare itself to the apple seed; the right fruit will arrive regardless. We may speak of an apple tree or a cherry tree, but to God this name does not matter. Creator creates and lets live freely, with no conditions, restrictions or expectations – just potential. Does the seed know of the existence of the tree within it? Does the tree know its full potential and how many fruits it will bear? God knows of the apple's existence before it was on the tree, of the apple tree before it was a tree, of the seed before it was a seed, and of the mother plant before it was a mother plant.

"I tell you truly, before Ibrahim came to existence, I am," Yeshua said. Why did he refer to Ibrahim in the past tense and to "I" in the present? If Yeshua existed before Ibrahim, than he should have referred to himself in the past, too. But the reference to Ibrahim is human and the reference to "I" is spiritual. *Before a divine emanation from God came to exist in human form – that the parents called Ibrahim – Spirit (Enana, I within I) exists (always or eternally).*

This was part of a conversation Yeshua had with those who argued that the authority of human Ibrahim was greater than that of human Yeshua. They argued that Ibrahim was a prophet and an elder to Yeshua, whose authority was therefore less than Ibrahim's. Yeshua tried to tell them that authority does not come from human (Ibrahim) but from Divine. That Spirit within himself (Enana) existed before the human form of Ibrahim was created. It was not Ibrahim they should listen to, but Spirit within Ibrahim, Yeshua and themselves; Ibrahim's human age in relation to Yeshua's is irrelevant.

So, when did the Enana in Ibrahim exist? When did the Enana in Yeshua exist? And when did the Enana in you exist?

Ibrahim, Yeshua, you, me and all of humanity – as emanations of the Creator – exist before we took a human form.

I remember when my niece Veronica was very young and being bothered by her baby brother Ryan. She got so bugged that she asked her mother, "Mum, how long will he be my brother for?"

My sister Blanche laughed. But now I ask a similar question, "For how long will Creator be our creator?" Should we laugh or ponder?

NINETEEN

MATTHEW'S SUPPORT

Days after the surgeon's follow-up, the oncology department phoned for an appointment to see Jonathan. Espy was worried. She didn't want Jonathan to go through the corridor that led to the signposted Sears Oncology Centre and neither did I. Jonathan did not want to go as well. I told them I would go alone and see what they said, but when I got there I became nervous. What would they say to me? They had already told us that neither chemotherapy nor radiation would benefit Jonathan.

When they realized Jonathan was not with me, they became a bit upset. The doctor didn't say anything, but it was evident they did not appreciate I had let Jonathan decide not to come.

"He is very apprehensive," I explained meekly. "I don't want to pressure and upset him."

"That's understandable," the nurse said, "but we needed to weigh him and see how he is doing."

I was told the report of findings after Jonathan's latest surgery was not in yet, but they did not think it would be any different from the diagnosis we'd already been given. I did my best not to show my feelings. "We have to tell him his diagnosis," the doctor said next.

"Why?"

"Because it is his body, not yours, and he needs to know what is going on with his body. I have been an oncologist for many years, and I know how to handle such issues. I have even had dying children ask their parents if they (the parents) would be okay."

"That is fine," I said, "but what is the purpose of killing someone before they are dead?" I will not forget the look on the doctor's face on hearing those words. It was as if I had not only lost my mind, but had lost it in transit from another planet.

From then on, things did not go well. The doctor interrupted whenever I tried to speak.

"If you don't tell him, how will you handle the guilt if he dies without knowing he has cancer?"

"Doctor," I heard myself say, "the Spirit is greater than the body. If what you say is true and science is telling us that Jonathan's body is going to die, then we have to care for his Spirit."

Again that look returned. "I have many patients in similar situations, Vince. Jonathan is a smart kid. I can assure you that he knows what he has. He has seen my badge, he has read the sign outside the clinic, and he has access to the internet, right?"

"Yes, he does."

"I guarantee you, he knows. I have this problem with another family and they too are Indian. I only have this issue with Indian families."

I was speechless.

"What about your wife and other son? What do they have to say about this?" Was I being told that I was forcing my way of thinking on the rest of the family?

"They feel the same way," I said. "Our belief is that Spirit is greater than the body, and if science and medicine can do nothing for Jonathan, it is our duty to ensure Spirit is cared for." There was no way I was going to give up easily.

"Look," the doctor said, "Jonathan qualifies for Children's Wish, and the whole family can go on a vacation and have a good time. Is there anywhere you would like to go?"

"Well, I had thought of going to Goa, but we don't know if Jonathan is strong enough to travel."

"This is the best he is going to be. You should go now. But we must tell him first and then initiate the process for Children's Wish."

Without thinking, this came out of me: "Doctor, I did not give him life. There is a higher being that gave Jonathan life. So I cannot tell him that his life will end. It is not my place to tell Jonathan of his death. The giver of his life will tell him."

Immediately the doctor replied, "You don't have to tell him. I will."

"What if it causes him anxiety and depression?"

"We have lots of things we can give him for that. In fact, at some stage everyone in your family may have to be on antidepressants."

"No!"

"Do you realize that you will have to live with guilt for the rest of your life?"

"If God decides to call Jonathan back, Jonathan will be given all knowledge, he will know and understand what I am doing and why. He will have all knowledge. He is my son, I know him very well and he knows me well, too. I am doing what I'm doing to protect him and out of my love for him. I feel no guilt. There is none and will never be."

To heck with this doctor. I had been a medical sales representative for many years, and ten years of my career had been in Goa, India. *I have friends there I can call and ask for an opinion on how to care for Jonathan.* I truly felt that this doctor did not care for my son, that the Shem was not right. *Espy, Matthew, I and the rest of the family, care and will care as we always have. We are the caregivers. The doctor is just a guide, a road sign; doctors give us a scientific opinion. We make the decisions, we sign the waivers. They don't.* Waivers absolve doctors of responsibility and place it on the patient or guardian. So who makes the decision and who the suggestion? To genuinely care for the patient involves more than just science, education, statistics, laws, protocol and logic. Care includes nurturing, kindness, understanding, patience, love and compassion; it must include Shem, Soul, Spirit, Atma, Being – our whole selves – that which God created, not just the mask that we have made ourselves to be.

The doctor realized that I was getting ready to leave the consulting room. "I would like to meet your other son Matthew and speak to him about this."

"Sure," I said.

"Is next Wednesday okay?"

"Yes, we will be here. Thank you, doctor."

On Monday the following week, the doctor called the house. I was out, and Espy took the call. The moment I got back, I could see from her face that something was wrong.

"The oncologist called," Espy said.

"Why?"

"About telling Jonathan ..." Espy could not continue.

"I had this discussion with the oncologist last week," I said. "I said we are dealing with it. Matthew and I have an appointment to see this doctor on Wednesday. Why this damn insistence on telling Jonathan he is going to die?"

By now, Jonathan had recovered so well that he had gone out to movies twice with his cousin Keane and once with a friend. He seemed so well. He had even played some badminton with me. I meditated and prayed for nearly two hours a day; so did Espy and our sisters, brother, friends and many well-wishers.

Playing backyard badminton.

I called the doctor from the park in front of our house so that Jonathan wouldn't hear the conversation. "Please," I implored, "if you need to talk to us, call me on my cell phone. I am always available, any time. It is very difficult for my wife to hear about the probable death of our son."

There was a pause. Then, "Vince, it is not a probability. Jonathan has hepatocellular carcinoma. It is terminal. I have the reports from the surgery."

My heart dropped. I couldn't speak and could hardly see through the tears. After some time, I managed, "Are you sure?"

"I am so very sorry, Vince, but the reports rule out the possibility of it being embryonic cell cancer, and so the original diagnosis stands."

"Is there anything else we can explore? What about alternative therapies?" I thought of my friend Rajni, who is associated with a researcher in the US who is working on a new drug to treat terminal cancers, and I told the doctor briefly about this experimental drug.

"We can look at it. If you have any information, email it to me and I will look at it. But this is hepatocellular cancer, Vince. You are talking about reversing something never reversed before."

"I would still like to look into it," I insisted.

"Okay, but if you don't let me tell Jonathan, it is unethical for me to administer him this experimental drug. Do you know what your wife said to me when I called her? She said, 'My stomach churns at the thought of telling my son he has cancer.' Well let me tell you something, Vince. It is my stomach that is churning at the thought of not telling him he has cancer."

"We have an appointment the day after tomorrow," I said. "Let's talk then." My mind was racing again. I leaned on a tree in the park. Then I sat on a bench. Then I was back at the tree as I tried to collect myself.

Espy loved watching Jonathan enjoy a good meal.

How do I tell Espy? What do I tell her? *Do* I tell her?

I did not want to go home. I hoped time would stand still. I hoped I would not need to do anything, but of course I had to. Espy knew I was talking to the oncologist. As soon as I walked in, she asked me what happened. I glanced at her and knew she read my Shem. She knew.

"But he is doing so well!" she cried.

"Espy, what can I say to you?" is all I managed. "Let's talk later. We have to maintain a good environment for Jonathan – that is the most important thing. We'll manage somehow. From now on we are not important. It is just Jonathan that matters, no one else. Nothing else. Just Jonathan."

After phoning Rajni for information on the experimental drug he had told me of, I emailed the oncologist. We would have difficulty importing it, as it was not approved in Canada.

I called all who were praying for Jonathan, bringing us food now and then, or just calling to talk with us. Everyone started praying even harder. We were still absolutely sure a miracle was happening. The medical professionals had said Jonathan was not likely to celebrate his seventeenth birthday, but I kept feeling he would be okay. He had recovered well from the last surgery and had now moved back into his own room. He had even gone out a few times. He went to school after hours a couple of times to meet his buddies and told me he really enjoyed that. When Espy and I got a chance to speak, we agreed we would continue to believe Jonathan was healed and the cancer would leave him.

Two days later, Matthew and I headed to SickKids Hospital to meet with the doctor. Jonathan's hepatologist and another doctor also came to this meeting. On the drive there, Matthew expressed concern about Jonathan not knowing his diagnosis. I explained that we were Jonathan's support system and that a support system is not just a phrase we say to make us feel good, it is actions we perform to help Jonathan. If a person is in crisis and our response is, "This is your body, and here's what's going on, and so now you have to deal with it," that is not support. That is actually avoiding responsibility and deserting the person in need.

When Yeshua realized his arrest was inevitable, he went to a garden to pray. He took a few friends with him, hoping for support from them. Instead, he found them asleep while he was in torment. "Can you not stay up an hour with me?" he asked. What was he looking for? For them to stay awake and just be with him. He knew his arrest was imminent. But he longed for a friend to be there, to hug him, maybe to walk a few steps with him, and maybe just to sit with him in silence.

We don't always know what to say and do for someone in a critical situation, especially if we don't have experience of dealing with such situations. But when a friend needs us, if we are a friend, we must be available. We have been told Jonathan is going to die shortly; we need to be here with him. We are his support system, aren't we? Then we have to take some of the load off him. If, in doing so, we are injured – mentally, emotionally or physically – then so be it. That is the price we pay for being a support system. We have to perform when the need arises. If we make him deal with the situation, what support have we provided him?

"If that is the route we are taking, Papa, then we go all in or nothing," Matthew said. "We go all spiritual or not at all."

"We go all spiritual, Matthew," I said with warmth and gratitude. His words warmed my heart and gave me strength.

"Great! Maybe afterwards you can take Joddu to India and try some of that Ayurvedic stuff." Ayurvedic medicine is one of the world's oldest holistic healing systems, developed in India thousands of years ago.

"Yes," I said. "He needs to get strong enough to travel to India, and I don't think he is yet."

"Yes, Papa. I didn't mean immediately. We should go as soon as Jonathan starts gaining strength to travel."

At the hospital, I introduced Matthew to the medical team, and after some pleasantries, we talked about Jonathan. The doctor spoke to Matthew, asking how much he knew about Jonathan's condition, how much he was involved, and what his thoughts were.

Matthew does not speak unnecessarily, but when he does, he is very specific. He spoke to the doctors with care and thought. "We are a very different family," he said, "and we are not really concerned with what others think of us. We do not walk hand in hand or sing Kumbaya, but we know and understand each other." He took a breath, looking at them to see if they understood. "We support each other. Now that we, along with Jonathan, are faced with this difficult task, we will do everything to help and support Jonathan."

Jonathan's graduation from elementary school.

Matthew was told about informing Jonathan of the

diagnosis and prognosis of his condition.

Matthew responded, "Our family's decision is not to inform him until it is absolutely necessary."

I stepped in to reinforce that we were Jonathan's support system and that we – his family – knew him better than anyone else, and this knowledge was prompting our decision. My comment was ignored and Matthew was asked to give an example of his relationship with his younger brother.

This is crazy, I thought. *We are not in a kindergarten class.* Matthew was getting upset as well, but he spoke of one time when Jonathan had confided in him about a girl at school who had a crush on him, and Jonathan had talked to Matthew for guidance on what to do.

"We had a nice brotherly talk," Matthew said, "and then went about our lives. That's it – nothing spectacular."

One of the doctors turned to me. "See? You say you know your son. Did you know he was interested in a girl?"

I was about to answer, but what would that have achieved? How could I prove I know my son to one who believed that "knowing" a person meant pinning down facts and events? My jaw dropped in bewilderment. How could I respond in a way that would be understood? I glanced at Matthew and saw heat building up in him. I couldn't let him say something that might turn up the heat in that small room, and so I brought up the issue of travel and the Children's Wish Foundation. We were not actually interested in travelling, mostly because Jonathan was not yet fit enough, but I wanted to let the tension dissipate.

Matthew said, "These material things do not interest us. If I asked Jonathan what he would really like after the rough time he has had for the past year, he would say, 'Let's have a nice steak and chill out.' Then we'd play video games or something."

"So what will you do when he starts displaying symptoms?" the doctor asked Matthew.

"I don't know right now, but we will figure it out when the time is right."

I needed to change the subject. "Is there anything we can do to make Jonathan better?" I asked.

"Well, I have told you this is definitely not embryonic cell cancer, it is hepatocellular cancer. There is no cure for this. We can give him some chemotherapy, but I do not believe it will benefit Jonathan. The chemotherapy will cause him to lose hair, get weak and present other side effects that far outweigh any benefits he may receive from it. And I will not give him chemotherapy unless he knows what his diagnosis is. But really, the chemotherapy will not do much for him. It may extend his life by a few weeks, but his quality of life will not be good."

"What about radiation?"

"I have to get a specialist to study Jonathan's case and give me a report on whether radiation will give him any benefit at all. It will not make the cancer go away, but there are no serious side effects with radiation, so it could give him a better quality of life towards the end. But I need to get a specialist to write me a report first, and I will not do that unless you commit now to giving Jonathan radiation if the report is favourable."

"Why so?" I asked.

"Well I am not going to waste a specialist's time writing a report if you are not going to give him the radiation."

"That's a threat!" I said.

Matthew jumped in. "Isn't this specialist paid by our tax money to do his job? Isn't Jonathan entitled to this opinion? Tell the specialist to do his job! We are not a waste of time, are we? Tell him to do his job!"

"No, no, please don't consider this a threat. It's not a threat. I'll be doing the report myself. I will do the report and get back to you. You decide then how to proceed," the doctor replied.

As we stepped out, Matthew was furious.

"Let's pray the doctor does the report, Matthew," I said.

TWENTY

THE MOMENT I KNEW

On the drive home that day, Matthew seemed to want to stay with his thoughts, and I was considering what to tell Espy and Jonathan. Though not fully fit and strong, Jonathan was doing well. Espy, Matthew and I believed that he would continue to improve and be well. Eventually, we would look at this experience as a bad dream. We believed this beyond a shadow of a doubt.

I did not tell Espy or Jonathan all the details of our meeting with the doctors. I just said it was okay and they would like to see Jonathan sometime soon.

"I am not going back," Jonathan said. "I don't want to go there ever again."

By the look in Espy's eye, I could tell she was concerned. Espy can read my Spirit – my Shem. We had decided there would be no talk of doom and gloom around Jonathan. If we could create an environment that was nurturing, kind, gentle, compassionate and loving, conducive to a godly environment, all would be well.

I had spoken to friends, and everyone believed a miracle was happening. But now this belief was hard to hold onto while listening to the doctors and thinking about what they were telling us. They were telling us what they saw and considered reality: the images from MRIs and CT scans, counts from pathology reports.

But we saw Jonathan well. My sisters, brother and all those praying saw him well. *Jonathan will be well. All is well.*

Jonathan continued to improve during the month of June, and I went back to work. I would call home several times a day to see how Jonathan was doing. My friend Rajni visited me at work and asked how Jonathan was.

"He is very well," I said.

"I worry about him and about you."

"Don't worry, Rajni, nothing will happen to him. He will be fine. I know he will be well."

"I have spoken to my friend who is conducting research on an experimental drug for terminal cancers –"

I cut him short. "Don't worry, Rajni. Jonathan does not have cancer. If he did, he is now healed. He is at home and improving very well."

Rajni has known me for a long time and knew that if I was convinced of something, nothing could change my mind. He is a practising pharmacist, so when I told him of Jonathan's diagnosis, he knew what the prognosis was. But my faith had erased the prognosis from my perception, and I was convinced of the miracle that was healing Jonathan.

"If any signs appear, please talk to me," he said kindly.

"Rajni, nothing will happen, no signs will appear. Jonathan is well."

"Okay. But just promise me that if anything happens, you will talk to me."

"I promise." But I had no doubt. So many people were praying, and the prayers had to have an effect. "Blessed are those who do not see yet believe," were Yeshua's words. I believed.

Then a strange thing happened. Jonathan began to experience stomach pain. Espy attributed this to his ulcerative colitis, but I recalled the oncologist telling me that this was one of the first terminal symptoms. Even though the pain was not severe, Jonathan said he'd like to sleep on our bed again for a few days until he felt better. We were glad to do that. I went into his room, and he slept with Espy in our room. After he had slept in our room for three days, I got a strange telephone call at work. When I walked in at around 9:00 a.m., my colleague Priscila came in and said, "I just had a call from Felix, and he really wanted to talk to you. He says he is from the same village as you and has not spoken to you for a long time. He would really like you to call him back."

"Felix from Calangute?"

"I could not catch the name of the place, but he said you are both from the same village."

I know three people named Felix, and two of them are from Calangute. I thanked Priscila and decided to call Felix back immediately. While I was in the kitchen to grab a coffee, it struck me. I did know Felix, he is from the northwestern side of my village. I had come to know of him moving to Canada through Angelo, a mutual friend, and Angelo had also informed me that Felix's young son had died in a road accident.

There are no coincidences. Like the seed whose development into a tree and the fruit it will give are planned by and known to God, God plans all occurrences, encounters, people, things, and thoughts on our journey. Tears welled. I could no longer see my cup as the coffee brewed, but somehow I managed to get the coffee, walk to my office, shut the door and sit down.

What am I being told? What are you saying? I asked God. Unable to speak, eyes brimming, I sat looking out the window. But I saw nothing, heard nothing, felt nothing. I saw no vision as Yeshua's father, Youssef, or Paul or Yohan the apostle had seen. I heard no booming voice as Ibrahim, Moses, Saul, Noah, and Lot are said to have heard. But in less than an instant I received a "knowing" that was so clear it shocked me to tears and grief.

This experience helped me to tell Jonathan later how God communicates and how he (Jonathan) would eventually communicate with us and with his family on the other side.

This is what I came to know: *Jonathan is going to die before his seventeenth birthday. There is nothing anyone will be able to do. His role is fulfilled, and the time for him to return home is at hand. While helping Jonathan prepare for this part of his journey, I should strengthen myself by learning from Jonathan and at the same time help Espy, Matthew, our extended family, friends and myself with the knowledge I receive from God and through Jonathan.*

Was it shock, grief, or God that made me stay still as I absorbed this? I do not know how long it took before I finally called Felix back.

"Hey! Vince, congratulations! How are you, man?"

"Congratulations?" I was dazed and puzzled. "For what?"

"Come on now, you don't have to be so humble. I saw the announcement that your company has moved to a big new location, and I'm very happy for you."

"Oh," I replied, "where did you see that?"

"It is posted on the Goan-news website – you don't know it's there?"

"No, we put it out on a business newswire, but I had no idea it was on the Goan-news site."

"I'll send you the link," Felix said. "We are all very happy for you and wish you all the very best. We haven't seen you for a long time, though, Vince. Come for the BMX function later this summer. We can catch up."

"No, Felix, my young son is not well ..." I was unable to continue.

Fortunately, Felix spoke immediately. "It's okay, look after family first, Vince. Your son is your priority. Kids are entrusted to us, and we have to fulfill our responsibility."

I was crying but could not let Felix know that, so I let him talk.

"How is your family?" I was able to ask at last.

"Well, I had three kids, but now I have only two."

"How are you dealing with that?"

"With great difficulty, man." He was choking. "It's six years and there is not a single day that I do not think of my son. God has helped us become stronger, though. We did not want to see, talk or meet anyone for a long time. But we are okay now, I guess. It is very painful. Barbara and I still cry, but we are stronger and a closer family now."

After we'd chatted a little longer, I managed to tell him I would call again later. I was not holding up, and I needed to collect myself.

TWENTY-ONE

"JONATHAN AND GOD HAVE A DEAL"

I stared out the office window hoping for something to happen, for someone to tell me Jonathan would not die. *Why does he have to die? Why not me? I am fifty-two, he is sixteen. Let him live. If I die, a few people will grieve and life may change for my wife, two sons and a few others. But Jonathan has not even lived yet. Let him get his driver's license, let him go out on a date. He wants a ride on Matthew's motorcycle. He wants to be a chef – let him, please. PLEASE! What will you or anyone gain from his death?* After many minutes of this, I began to realize that another thinking was happening alongside this thinking.

The other thinking was this: What am I trying to do? How can I change God's plan? Is it me that made the plan, or God? How can I decide the time of Jonathan's death, or mine for that matter? If I were Creator, I could redo the plan if I so wished. Isn't asking Creator to change the plan the same as asking Creator to follow my plan? Is this not an attempt to humanize God? Yet, I have heard that if we are loyal or pleasing to God, we will be rewarded with a long life. We are told that God does not bring us to a certain stage, whether in life, in business or in health, to destroy us. That God tries and tests us with tribulations only to rescue us, even at the last second. How can anyone say that Jonathan has been disloyal or done anything to displease God? Matthew, Espy and I have known him since he was born. He gave me no reason to punish or shout at him even once; a sentence or two to correct him were all that was needed. So what could he have done that was so displeasing that a good, kind and compassionate God insists – despite so many prayers – on ending Jonathan's life?

Nothing. Absolutely nothing was the answer then as now. This was Jonathan's mission: he was designed by God to travel this earth for a human-measured timespan of sixteen years, eight months and thirteen days.

I remembered the words my nephew Ryan had said to his mother Blanche (my sister) when I told her of Jonathan's diagnosis in May, 2014.

"Don't cry, Mum," Ryan had said. "Jonathan and God have a deal."

"A deal?" Blanche asked.

"Yes," Ryan continued. "A long time ago, God and Jonathan had a talk, and God told Jonathan that God needs Jonathan to visit Aunty Espy and Uncle Vincent and live with them for some time. But God said, 'It will be only a short time, and then you have to come back. Deal, Jonathan?' And Jonathan replied, 'Yes, deal.' Jonathan cannot break that deal, Mum. He has to go back – that is the deal they made."

How do children know such things? Yeshua said, "I praise you, Father, Lord of heaven and earth, because you have hidden these things from the wise and learned, and revealed them to little children."

Now, Ryan was twenty-two, so not exactly little, but his mind was innocent, not crowded with science, justifications and excuses. A child-like mind easily accepts that it doesn't know the plan of God and therefore is willing to observe the plan as it unfolds. It does not proclaim that God is good and will cure or perform miracles if we fulfill certain conditions. These may happen, but really we do not know. We can assume, we can believe, we can expect ... but we do not know.

How is it that children are more accepting of God's plan than adults are? Is it that the longer we live, the more we ask God to follow our own plans? Do we come to expect a certain lifespan for ourselves and our children? We plan, we train them, we encourage them to become doctors, priests, lawyers and politicians. How do we know if that is what God has planned for them? If we take an apple seed and plant it in a mango grove, will it bear mangoes? Jonathan was not born with a guarantee of a certain number of years. If he had been, there would be no need to take him to hospital. The guarantee would assure us that Jonathan's time was not done, and so he would not die. None of us is given such a guarantee. We named him Jonathan Anthony Leitao and assumed he would outlive his parents, just as I had outlived mine and Espy had outlived her father. Are we looking to God to endorse our expectations?

Our life, path and the experiences therein are planted and nurtured by God our Creator, who speaks to us through the eternal communion between Creator God and created Spirit. We do in fact have a very long life, as our Spirit lives eternally. Sometimes our earthly expectations for long human life and wealth coincide with the plan of God, but we should always know that the plan of God precedes human expectations. As a sailor sets his sails according to the wind, so must we set our expectations according to God's plan, and be continually vigilant of the Will and plan of God as the sailor is of the wind. Without knowing the direction of the wind, the sailor cannot set his sail, so how can we accept something without knowing what it is? If we first assume we know God's plan and accept it, we are at risk of accepting an untruth and then – when the real plan unfolds – becoming confused, angry, and disillusioned.

By creating our own plan, we assume a position where we create and then expect God to accept and endorse our plan. We attempt to perform the function of the Creator and replace Creator with creation. In the Psalms this is referred to as pasha.

In ancient India, a story was told of a simple, kind and wise man who was travelling with his friends. Suddenly he was confronted by someone who didn't agree with things he had said and who decided to give him a piece of his mind. The enraged man threw everything including the kitchen sink at him, but the simple man was not perturbed in the least. In fact, he was smiling, almost as if he were being told a joke. Once the assault was over, the simple man continued his journey with a broad smile. "How is it you are not upset?" his friends asked. He replied, "If someone is giving you a gift, and you do not accept it, who has it?" The simple man in this story was Siddharta Gautama, later known as the Buddha. God has a plan for us and offers it to us, but if we keep insisting that it be changed, who then has God's great plan?

TWENTY-TWO

ACCEPTING GOD'S PLAN

As June drew to an end, Jonathan's stomach pains were slowly growing worse. How could this be? I didn't want to believe that Jonathan could be dying.

So many people are praying, we are praying, I have heard of so many miracles happening. A pastor prophesied to a friend that "a young boy who has liver cancer was touched by the Lord and healed. The pastor was not prompted," he said, "and did not even know Jonathan had cancer." Despite this, every day Jonathan displayed more terminal signs. Should I believe the prophecies? Should I believe the scriptures, the holy men and their sermons, the priests, evangelists, friends, God? Whom do I believe?

I believed Jonathan was healed. Everyone told me to have faith. A pastor prophesied, and a friend conveyed that message to me. But my senses were now confirming what I had come to know directly from God in my office the day I received the telephone message to call back Felix: that Jonathan would die before his seventeenth birthday. Who was wrong? Was it me, my sisters, brother, family, friends, pastor or priests? If someone was lying, how could I believe them again?

Preachers tell us miracles happen if we only believe. Who can tell me that I did not believe, that I do not believe? Yet my human senses, designed by God, were gathering information that Jonathan's terminal symptoms were becoming more and more prominent, that his bodily health was deteriorating daily. I spoke to a dear friend and told him, "I have to accept God's plan as it unfolds. I do not know what it is yet. I believed this was a test for me and for Jonathan and that the test would be over and he would not die. But now it is too obvious. The doctors estimated he would live for four to nine months from May. Now I have to accept that I cannot go on believing Jonathan will be healed."

"I am very disappointed with you for giving up," he scolded me. "How can you give up on your own son? God will never give up on him. I will not and neither should you."

I spoke to two others: one a good friend and another a relative. "Don't worry, we will storm heaven for Jonathan's life," they both assured me.

Their words and reactions perturbed me deeply. How could anyone think I would give up on my son? And how can anyone say, "God will never give up on him?" Do you know the thought of God and what God has planned for my son, for me, and for you? Do you assume you know God's plan and that your assumption is the truth? Those who storm heaven, please explain to me what you mean by that. Do you go with a petition to heaven along with an army of the faithful who fast, do penance and pray continually to force God to accept your plan and forsake the original one?

To some, this may seem a joke or just a story. To me and my family, this was our path we walked it. Experiencing every single moment, sometimes without anyone knowing what it felt like to be struck by – what seemed like – multiple lightning bolts at the same time, to be told Jonathan had liver cancer, that he would die in a short while, that there is no hope for him ... Every moment was unique, and we did not know what would happen to Jonathan or to any of us in the next moment. Even the doctors could offer us no certainty. In May, they told us Jonathan would live for four to nine months. As it turned out, he lived three months and three weeks from the day they told us. How could we plan or know what was next? How could we believe everything would be okay, that Jonathan would have a decent quality of life in his final days? Could we ask God to take away Jonathan's pain? Through the previous few months, our track record in asking God to do this or that for Jonathan had not been good. So what were we to do?

Nothing, absolutely nothing. Just observe, watch, help, and "be here," as Jonathan had asked me to in the x-ray room. Being present to the events as they unfold from God's plan at each inevitable moment is the only way to accept God's plan. God's plan or Will is with us here and now, not in the past or the future. We plan the future and ask God to endorse these plans, or we worry about the past and ask God to help us; but neither the past nor the future is here. Now is the moment that Jonathan and all of us have been offered by our Creator. The question to ask is this: if we do not accept Creator's offering of this moment, who will have it?

TWENTY-THREE

"I DON'T FEEL GOOD, MAMA"

We were still resolved not to tell Jonathan that he was going to die until it became obvious and necessary. My conviction was still strong that if medicine and science could not save Jonathan, then it was our duty to care for and help Spirit in him to move on. Every time I told the oncology team this, the looks I got seemed to say, "Oh! This guy is some Indian snake charmer who thinks he can charm Jonathan's spirit into a trance. We need to medicate him!"

We have studied the human body, its parts and organs, its features and functions, but have very little knowledge of Spirit. If we accept data only from the human senses and convince ourselves that what we cannot perceive is unreal, than how can we accept the existence of Spirit? If we cannot accept the existence of this eternal being (Spirit), then we are like a tiny ant in front of an elephant. The ant sees only what is in the scope of its vision and therefore will conclude elephants do not exist. That is why some educated and well practised scientists cannot accept that Spirit is bigger than the body. The human is provided with senses to help us survive in this material realm. Without the senses, we would stumble and fall or burn ourselves. But it is human stupidity that persuades us that what the senses cannot perceive does not exist. There are colours the human eye cannot see, yet we know they exist. How then do we persuade ourselves that Spirit does not exist?

Our human senses cannot verify Spirit: it has no shape, size, smell, taste, feel or sound. No memory of Spirit can be stored in human memory. How then can we recognize Spirit? When Yeshua realized his arrest was inevitable, his friends failed him. In critical situations, our human intelligence, education, culture, friends and pastors will also fail us. But that which is within – Enana, the "I" within "I" – is always there, Enana never fails. Before the human was created, I (Enana, Spirit, Atma, Soul, Shem or Spirit) exist, God exists, and I emanate from God. So I (Enana) am still standing. *Enana urha shrara wa hayye.* Aramaic words of Yeshua translate as: "The 'I' within 'I' is the way, the truth and the life." Now Spirit is in communion with God.

In the second week of July 2014, it became clear that Jonathan was beginning to get a sense he was seriously ill.

"I don't feel good, Mama," he said. "Something is not right. I feel this is the end for me."

Espy did her best not to cry, and she remained strong. She told us later, "If he saw me cry, he would panic and do the same." She remained strong so Jonathan could draw strength from her. She was tired, drained by this journey we were on. Jonathan would wake up often at night, and during the day we would be there for whatever he needed. But though she was physically exhausted, she held strong. Even now, I cannot fully express how strong she was. I cried often, but she held up very bravely.

"No, Joddu, you will be fine. There have been many times you've been unwell and you always bounce back," she told him.

"It's not like that now, Mama. This time it's different."

By the middle of July, we needed to increase the morphine dosage. Jonathan argued with the doctors, saying that morphine was not good – he'd learned about it in school – and he didn't want to get addicted to it. He fought and tolerated the pain as much as he could, refusing to take morphine until he could no longer bear the pain.

It seemed to me that Jonathan's thinking had changed drastically. He spoke less and was pensive, almost sage-like. He chose his words very carefully.

"Something is not right," he said. "I think this is it for me. Nothing is working."

I had said to the doctors, "I did not give him life. There is a higher being that gave Jonathan life. So it is not my place to tell Jonathan of his death. The giver of his life will tell him." They had looked at me as if I had lost my mind. But now Jonathan knew. Maybe not the whole story, but he was beginning to get an understanding. Was Spirit in Jonathan's body receiving communication and wisdom from Divine Creator?

TWENTY-FOUR

RADIATION AND A STRANGER'S COMPASSION

By the third week of July, we knew we had to tell Jonathan of his diagnosis and imminent death. His stomach had begun to protrude, and he was having difficulty swallowing food. He was low on energy and would become extremely tired without doing anything. On the seventeenth of July, Jonathan had an appointment with Dr. Simon Ling, his liver specialist at SickKids Hospital. The oncologist had offered to meet Espy and Jonathan at the liver clinic for a short consultation. Jonathan lacked energy and did not want to come.

"It's no use, Mama. Nothing is working. I am too tired and don't want to go." Espy pleaded with him, and to please her, he finally agreed. He was asked if he wanted to be included in doctors' meetings and discussions regarding his treatment.

"Just talk to my parents, it's fine," Jonathan said. After the meeting with Dr. Ling, the three of us waited in vain for the oncologist. When we contacted the clinic, we were told to bring Jonathan to the oncology clinic at the other end of the hospital.

"Doctor, you said you would meet us at the liver clinic," Espy begged. "Jonathan is too tired to come all the way to the other end of the hospital." But it made no difference. So again she pleaded with Jonathan, this time to agree to be wheeled to the other end of the hospital. When we got there at last – Jonathan was exhausted – we were told that the specialist's report was completed and that Jonathan would be given five doses of radiation. This information could have easily been given to us over the phone.

When did protocol become more important than compassion?

We were reminded that radiation is not a cure and that the tumours would grow again. "When they do, we cannot give him more radiation. This is not a cure. This may give him a bit of an improvement in the quality of his life after a few days. When the tumour regrows, there is nothing we can do." Espy could not handle this, which is why whenever possible I would talk to the doctors while she and Jonathan waited outside.

Espy did everything she could and more to ensure Jonathan was showered with love and held in loving care, and then more loving care, and then even more. This was our only concern, to fill our hearts with love so that the Spirit within Jonathan would perceive that the "I" within "I" is love, and that he could lean on the love that surrounded him through Espy, Matthew and me. We felt this was what would nourish Jonathan and bring him peace.

Jonathan had to have another scan so they could mark the area that was to receive radiation. On the drive home, he was exhausted and very quiet. At one point he was so tired he asked me to stop the car and let him rest from the motion of the car. I pulled into Fairview Mall, and as we stopped, he surprised me by asking for a spring roll. I hesitated – a spring roll is deep fried – but then I thought, what difference will it make now? He has always eaten healthy food, yet he is at death's door. He enjoyed that spring roll.

Radiation was set to be administered over five days. Espy was petrified and so was I, but we had to take him. Jonathan did not want to go, even when we told him the lumps in his liver needed to be shrunk so he would feel better.

"It's no use," he insisted. "It will not work. I just know it will not work."

"Please Joddu, let's do this. You will feel better."

"I'm too tired. I don't want to go there. I am done with the hospital – I just want to be home."

Eventually, and very reluctantly, Jonathan agreed to go. The radiation clinic was at Princess Margaret Cancer Centre in Toronto, a place I had never been. As I drove Jonathan and Espy to the centre, my life was not in me. I kept thinking, how long will we have Jonathan with us? It was now the end of July, and I could tell Jonathan would not live to see his seventeenth birthday in December. He had no energy. Even though he was eating a bit and having meal supplements, he had lost a lot of weight. As I drove on the Don Valley Parkway heading to the hospital, the blue vastness of Lake Ontario was in view ahead of me.

Would it be better if I just drove into the lake right now? The trauma would be much less for all of us. Except Matthew, he's not in the car. It would be horrible for Matthew. I managed to get this out of my head, but the thought returned two or three times. I felt if we all died together, Jonathan would have company and so would Espy and I. We could continue looking after Jonathan and would never be separated from him.

As I approached the hospital, the sign Princess Margaret Memorial Cancer Centre made my heart sink, or was it Shem within me that sank? I glanced at Jonathan and quickly made a u-turn to go to the rear entrance. I looked at him again, relieved that he seemed not to have noticed. But I was wrong; he told me later he did notice.

The radiologist was kind and respectful. He asked me what we had told Jonathan. "I will respect the wishes of the family," he assured us.

I said we had told Jonathan he has lumps in his liver that need to be shrunk. I asked him not to mention the word cancer.

"Oh, I have no problem with that," he said. "I have no problem saying lumps, and I promise you I will not utter the cancer word in my conversations with him. If this is the wish of the family, I am absolutely fine with it and will honour it."

I was stunned and bewildered. How could one doctor say Jonathan would not be given radiation if he was not told of his cancer, when this doctor has no issues at all about it? The two hospitals are a few blocks from each other. Are we not in the same health care system? Something needed to be corrected, but now was not the time to tackle that. Now was the time to focus on Jonathan.

Espy, her brother Proto, her sister Ana and I accompanied Jonathan to the radiation therapy centre. The room felt intimidating, with its clinical atmosphere and large, unfamiliar equipment, but the staff were compassionate, kind and accommodating. They knew Jonathan's prognosis and were gentle and understanding; they did all they could to make him and us comfortable. Ana found the situation difficult and had to step outside; the rest of us stayed until we were asked to leave to permit the treatment to be administered. Espy prayed with Jonathan and gave him a special blessing. I held his hand and spoke quietly to him. As we were leaving the room, I pointed to the screen from which Jonathan could see us in the waiting room outside. "I will be right outside, Joddu, I will be watching you from the screen outside, and you can watch me back on this screen. I'll be back as soon as it is done."

Jonathan nodded. I think he didn't speak because he would have cried, and knowing I would as well, he wanted to seem strong. Espy couldn't watch the screen. Proto and Ana sat beside her, and I stood by the screen, determined to be with Jonathan no matter what. A nurse came by and put her arm around me, the tears in her eyes mirroring mine. I felt her heart soften as she spoke soothingly. I didn't register her actual words, but I (Enana) perceived that she cared, that she felt my pain and willingly shared it. I did not have to ask or pray for her to help me. She just did it. How is it that some people are willing to feel your pain, go beyond what their job asks of them and become involved in your heartache despite the personal cost? And how is it that others do not call or visit and stay away or leave you alone?

And when she cared and reached out to me, I felt her take some of my pain away. Was this Spirit, within her and me? Did she feel my pain as I had felt Jonathan's in the x-ray room? She must have, or such a response would not have flowed from her. I do not know her name, but Spirit in me knows her Shem and Spirit in her knows mine. Our Shem is absolutely the same.

As the two passersby did in the Good Samaritan story, many people choose to look the other way when someone is in trouble. I know many did during our last few weeks with Jonathan here on earth. One of my relatives argued with my sister because of how she was praying for Jonathan and for us and said, "I don't like what you are doing. I will never forgive you if these bad things they are going through cause something to happen to your kids."

Another friend was reported to have said that he and his family were staying away from us because "God's punishment for sin is death."

Still others told me, after Jonathan had died, that they did not visit or even call us during Jonathan's terminal phase or even after his death because, "You are a very private person, Vince. If you were not so private, I would be there. I blame you for that." Really? If I am such a private person, how is it that we are friends?

Yet this lady beside me, a health care worker who had probably seen and cared for hundreds of patients with cancers similar to the one that was killing Jonathan, was standing with her arm around my shoulder, letting me lean on her, holding a tissue box in the other hand and crying as if Jonathan were her child. This is Divine Love.

"Look, your mother and brothers are outside looking for you," someone said to Yeshua.

"Who are my mother and my brothers?" was Yeshua's reply. "Whoever does the will of God is my mother and sister and brother."

The Spirit present in this lady is my sister, my brother, my mother, and my father – and it is also me. For we are all one: Spirit, Soul, Shem, Atma created by God in God's own likeness. One does not have to grab a microphone and shout, "Jonathan, Vince, I love you!" to express love. Love is present when you feel another's pain and joy. This is what Yeshua was trying to tell us when he said, "Love your neighbour as yourself." We have changed that to say, "Love your neighbour as you love yourself." But this is not what Yeshua said. What he meant is, you can only love another as yourself if you and your neighbour are one and the same being. This is why the lady beside me was crying: she could feel what I was feeling, she felt my heart or the core of my being shatter, and she stood by me to help. There was no pomp, no press reporters, no pastor to preach about it later, just her in full knowledge that another creation of God was in anguish and she responding with love. Such Divine Love makes us all one.

TWENTY-FIVE

DO NOT RESUSCITATE?

The radiation treatment seemed to last an eternity, even though it was only a few minutes. As soon as it finished, we rushed in to hold Jonathan's hand and help him off the bed into the wheelchair, anxious to get him home. We had to wait a bit, as he wanted some chips and juice.

While we were at the Princess Margaret, Dr. Christine Newman and members of her Palliative Care team came from SickKids to see Jonathan and us. First, they spoke compassionately to Jonathan. Then, in private, Dr. Newman spoke to me in detail about the balance of the radiation treatments. I took the opportunity to ask her about the "Do Not Resuscitate" (DNR) order we'd been advised to make in case of a 911 emergency. A week earlier, the oncologist had said, "We do not resuscitate such patients, Vince. I will give you a letter to hand to the 911 paramedics, and they will then know not to resuscitate Jonathan."

This concerned and confused me. I asked my sister, a pharmacist, but she did not know. She suggested I talk to Narcissa, a nurse and a dear friend to us and Jonathan. Narcissa did not have an answer, and another nurse I asked was also dumbfounded. And, to my horror, one late evening a few days after we were told about the DNR order, Jonathan complained of chest pain and breathlessness and asked me to call 911. The phone was in my hand, but I hadn't yet received the letter for the paramedics. What was I to do? If I called 911 and the paramedics arrived, they would resuscitate him. Then what? I panicked. Phone in hand, I tried to convince Jonathan to come with me to the hospital.

"I'll drive you, Joddu. We will have to explain the whole medical history to the paramedics, so let's just go to the hospital – they know your history."

"No, call 911," said Jonathan. As I did my best to unfreeze and dial 911, he said, "No ... no wait, it's okay, I think I'm better. The pain is gone and I can breathe. Maybe it was gas or something."

There I was, not knowing why he should not be resuscitated and not having the document to instruct the paramedics. If they had attended Jonathan, I might have had to watch them resuscitate him, knowing it wasn't supposed to be done, but not knowing why.

Now, with Dr. Newman, I asked her why a DNR was recommended. She explained that resuscitation is hard on patients in Jonathan's condition. It would probably crush his ribs and cause him a lot of pain; and, even if he recovered, he might survive only another two or three days at most. This was later explained to me again by Dr. Berger when he visited Jonathan at home.

"He would experience a lot of pain, Vince," she said kindly.

"But this is our choice, right?"

"Of course it is, Vince. No one can force you not to resuscitate Jonathan." Dr. Newman also explained that Jonathan's breathlessness could have been a blood clot dislodging and entering his circulatory system. That scared me, because I didn't know what to do.

"In view of your concerns, would you like to have the follow-up with the same oncologist once the radiation is complete?"

"I have no issues with that, Doc," I said, but then I got uncomfortable. "On second thought, I feel unsure this oncologist has our best interest in mind."

"It is a miscommunication, Vince. Let me handle this for you. I will ensure Jonathan has a different oncologist. You don't worry about any of this now. Jonathan needs you. If you want to take this up, you may do it, but do it later. Now is the time to focus on Jonathan." Assuring us of her support and availability, Dr. Newman left us to take Jonathan home from Princess Margaret Centre.

Jonathan experienced no side effects from the initial radiation, for which we were grateful. However, he resisted going for more treatments, certain that it was not going to benefit him. Every day he did not want to go, and every day with great difficulty Espy managed to persuade him to go. I wasn't able to talk him into it; but Espy's nurturing mother essence spoke to him. However, on the last day of radiation, before the treatment, he was angry with us.

"No more private meetings with the doctors, Mama. You heard right, Pa? I want to be at all the meetings with the doctors from now on. I want to know everything. No secrets, no whispering, I want to know everything."

"Okay, Joddu," I said with some trepidation.

"You promise?"

"Yes, Jonathan."

On the strength of this promise, he came for the last treatment.

By now, I had discussed with Dr. Newman that it was time to tell Jonathan of his illness and of his approaching death. She was going to speak to him, and I wanted to brief her first. So, after the last radiation treatment, I told Jonathan about this meeting Espy and I had arranged with Dr. Newman at her office at SickKids that we needed to finish, and then she would talk to him. After this there would be no more private meetings.

He was not happy. "I thought we would not have any more private meetings, Pap?"

"This one was arranged last week, Joddu. Let us just finish it, please. It won't be more than ten minutes. She will just brief me on the treatments and we'll be done. Uncle Proto will be with you. Mama is already with Dr. Newman, just ten minutes."

"Okay, never mind," he said. "I hope there will not be more."

As I left the room, I promised him there would not be.

Espy had already explained to Dr. Newman, and to Nora, Gurjit and the rest of the palliative care team how Jonathan was now asking questions that indicated he knew he was seriously ill.

"Last night Jonathan said to me, 'Look at my body. It is not co-operating, Mama. I want to know everything so that I can prepare myself in case it is something bad.' He wants to know everything about his health, his treatment and what his options are. He now wants to be involved in decisions," Espy told them.

As I entered the room, I felt that Jonathan did not really want to hear his diagnosis or prognosis; but rather, he wanted confirmation of what he already knew. The previous night, I had looked into his eyes when he said he wanted to prepare himself "in case it is something bad." He had looked straight into mine, and we both knew that he knew. He did not want to use the words "in case I die," because he knew Espy and I were not reconciled with his approaching death. Of course he did not want to accept it, of course he did not want to die. Human instinct is to live, to save itself and survive.

But what happens when we realize and accept the inevitability of our death?

TWENTY-SIX

"THERE IS NO NEED TO WHISPER IN SECRET"

Every moment of our lives is inevitable. Even so, humans try to avoid the inevitable by running away or by numbing ourselves through distraction, alcohol or drugs. Yet the inevitable moment occurs, with or without our acknowledgment of it. We have a choice: to ignore and remain in oblivion, or to accept and be aware and conscious. At a young age, Jonathan chose the latter. This isn't something he was trained to do; we had never discussed it. Yet rather than follow the crowd and run away from or fight the inevitable, sixteen-year-old Jonathan chose to accept, be aware, be conscious, let go and let happen. Spirit within him then took over and guided him the rest of the way, as you will see.

In our family, we do not regularly display affection and place flowers, gifts, cards and the like in each other's way. But our actions towards one another speak our love. And although sometimes we do bring flowers, gifts and so forth, they are an addition, not the standard. The standard is what's prompted by the core of our being, by Spirit and love.

Whatever has happened is a memory, and whatever is going to happen is not yet reality. Reality is what is happening at this moment. Jonathan observed his body, and that moment by moment he was getting sicker and sicker. Rather than resist and fight, he chose to accept, let go and let it happen. Did he now see "the plan" as it unfolded for him in each inevitable moment? Did he realize that whatever was to happen in the next moment was going to happen, and that there was nothing he, his earthly family or the medical professionals could do about it? And is that why he just observed himself and those around him? Is this why he felt no anguish even at the last moments of his life on earth?

I feel, realizing inevitability, observing "the plan" as it unfolded, accepting and letting go at the age of sixteen must have been difficult for Jonathan. Yet he seemed to have done it with ease. When I looked at him, he seemed pensive and sometimes a little sad, but not distressed and not anguished. He was just there. No comment, no objection, no frustration, no demanding why, and most importantly no anger at all.

For about three nights during the radiation treatment he experienced nightmares, but he did not need antidepressants, as was predicted by a health care professional. At this stage, I am certain Jonathan knew he was going to die and could have told us that, but I am even more certain he did not have the heart to break ours.

Perhaps he knew we would try to deny it and distract him, as we had so often done, hoping not to cause him hurt. He told Espy, "It's no use, Mama. Nothing is working. You guys are doing everything. Anything that can be done, you have done."

Is this why he did not want to go through the radiation treatments? I think he knew the doctors had told us of his prognosis. He said to Espy, "Papa is sniffing all the time. I know he is crying. And you guys are secretly whispering in brown language." I tell you for sure Jonathan knew.

Dr. Chris looked up as I came in. (Dr. Newman had invited us to call her "Chris," and we settled on calling her Dr. Chris.) "Let's finish off here and go be with Jonathan," she said. "We don't want him to get anxious." What an absolutely right thing to say at that moment! I was beginning to get anxious, too, and wanted to be with Jonathan who I was sure wanted to be with us.

In Aramaic, the word *touveyhoun* means divinely attuned and perfectly ripe at this very moment. In Dr. Chris was the thought that Jonathan needed us to be with him, and as she acted on it, I realized the same thought was in me and Espy as well. Dr. Chris's thought and action were perfectly in harmony with the Divine Spirit.

She could have said, "Let me make the parents understand first. I have to ensure they are calm and settled, and Jonathan can call us or his uncle will let us know if he gets troubled or anxious. If he asks for me, I am just in the next room. I'll be with him in a second." But she did not. She acted without interfering with the prompt of Spirit. This is "acting from the heart," from Divine Love. Just as the physical heart is the source of life and nourishment for all parts of the body, so also Spirit is the eternal source of life, love and compassion. And this Spirit is our real self. *Enana urha shrara wa hayye.* The "I" within "I" is the way, the truth and the life.

In the Bhagavad Gita, it is said, "He sees truly who sees the Supreme Lord present equally in all."

"If you do great things but have not love, you are but a gong and a cymbal." We heard a lot of gongs and cymbals through our journey with Jonathan, but we experienced love from Dr. Chris Newman, Gurjit, Nora, Rebecca and PACT (Paediatric Advanced Care Team) at SickKids Hospital in Toronto. Not only Jonathan, Matthew, Espy and I but our eternal Spirits are eternally grateful to them. They are *touveyhoun*. Also *touveyhoun* are the nurse from the Princess Margaret who put her arm around me, Dr. Berger and his team who looked after Jonathan in his last days, and nurse Elena who visited Jonathan at our house twice a day until he went home.

Back in the room where Jonathan was waiting, Dr. Chris sat down beside him. "Jonathan, your parents tell me that you now want to know everything about what is ailing you and what is going on with you and your body, is this right?"

He nodded, a big smile on his face. "Yes," he said. "There is no need to whisper in secret. We should all talk together. We are one family, we are a team, we must all know the same thing."

Who is saying this? My son Jonathan?

Dr. Chris spoke gently. "Okay, Jonathan, Gurjit and I will come to your house the day after tomorrow, and I promise you there will be no secrets between us. I will tell you the truth, and you can ask me any question and I promise to tell you the truth. Is that a deal?"

He was tired, yet he beamed, his big perpetually surprised eyes sparkling. He thanked Dr. Chris and Gurjit as we left for home. This was the last time Jonathan visited SickKids Hospital.

TWENTY-SEVEN

"YOU ARE GOING HOME, JONATHAN"

How do you tell a sixteen-year-old that he is dying?

On the appointed day, the seventh of August 2014, Dr. Chris Newman and Gurjit Sangha, a clinical nurse specialist, arrived at our house. By now I knew Dr. Chris liked coffee, so I brewed some, which she graciously complimented. Jonathan was comfortably settled in our bedroom, and the conversation started casually about the weather and basketball, but we knew why they were here and I was anxious. I wanted Jonathan to be handled gently, carefully, tenderly as we would handle him. But is there a "nice" or loving way to give him this information? *God, where are you? The Bible is full of stories where you send angels to announce things, or boom through the clouds, drop manna, part the sea ... can you show up, please? Just once for my young boy, whom I've only just started calling "young man." Can you, please? Just once, and never again will I ask. I promise, never again.* I was brought back from my thoughts as Dr. Chris began to speak.

"Jonathan, we came here to your home, to tell you the truth, as we promised you at your last visit to the hospital. We will keep that promise to you and will tell you all you want to know." She paused to look at Espy and me. We knew what would be next. Jonathan had had a troubled night, no nightmare, but disturbed sleep. Dr. Chris continued, "We want you to know that we are here for you. We will tell you all you want to know. If at any time you feel we are telling you too much, or if you feel that you have heard enough and want us to stop, we would like you to give us a sign so that we can stop. At this sign, I will stop talking and we will do whatever you wish us to do. If you want us to leave the room, we will do that. If you want us to stay, that will be okay too. Is that okay with you, Jonathan?"

He nodded.

"So what is the sign you will give us?" asked Dr. Chris gently. Strangely, I felt more peaceful now than when Dr. Chris and Gurjit had entered the bedroom.

Jonathan was holding a comfort pillow on his lap. "How about I just hold up this pillow?" he said.

"That is fine, Jonathan. The moment you hold up your pillow, I will stop."

Did he know? How much does he know? How will he handle this? What is going on in my boy's young mind? I wished I could have traded places with him.

"Jonathan," Dr. Chris continued, "you have been sick for a while now, and I am sure you are wondering what is going on. In fact, that is what you have told us you want to know. We have been telling you that you have lumps in your liver, is that right?" Jonathan nodded. "In medicine, we call this cancer, Jonathan, –"

Jonathan held up his pillow. He fell onto his left side on the bed and started crying. Dr. Chris stopped speaking. She and Gurjit had tears in their eyes.

"Would you like us to leave, Jonathan?" she asked.

He nodded, and Dr. Chris and Gurjit left to wait in the sitting room downstairs. Espy and I hugged Jonathan and cried with him. Slowly, he tried to speak to us. "I knew it, Mama," he said through tears. "I just knew it." It took him about twenty minutes to regain his composure. Then he sat up. "When the doctor called

Papa to say it may be a misdiagnosis, I knew right then something was seriously wrong." Then he wept again. I was sitting on the bed beside him. He rested his head on my shoulder and said, "Am I done, Papa? Is this it? Am I done?"

How could I tell him? I knew the answer, I had seen the signs, but how could I tell him?

"I don't know, Joddu," I faltered. "Let me call them back in."

Oftentimes I regret having said that. Jonathan trusted me. He knew I wouldn't lie to him, and yet he knew I would sometimes not tell him everything so as not to hurt him. I think he knew he "was done," but I think he also knew that this was one of the times I was not going to tell him everything. Should I have told him then? In what words do you tell your son he will die soon? Why did those words not form? On many other occasions, words popped out of me without me making an effort. Why did this not happen this time?

He agreed immediately to call in Dr. Chris and Gurjit. "So what happens now?" he asked them as they walked in.

"Well, Jonathan, from our side we will do everything to make sure that all your needs are met. We are going to arrange for a nurse to visit you twice a day, and a doctor will come and see you every day as well. It is our understanding, and your parents have told us, that you would like to be at home."

Jonathan listened quietly and intently to this. Dr. Chris continued, "The type of cancer you have is very rare, Jonathan, and it will eventually take your life. When exactly this will happen, we do not know, and no one can tell that for sure. We promise you, Jonathan, that we will do everything we can – and there is a lot we can do – to ensure that the remainder of your life will be as good as possible. There are medications we will ensure are in your room, available to you, that will make life easier for you."

Jonathan had big sparkling eyes that we all loved. His eyebrows were naturally raised, as if he were permanently surprised or inquiring. Often we teased him about this, but it was his natural expression. Now, with this expression, he looked first at his mum, then at me, then at the doctor, then at Gurjit, and then back to us, searching for our response. I cannot say how we were responding at that moment. We wanted to be strong for him, so he could draw strength, comfort, peace, love, compassion, empathy and understanding from us. Did he? I don't know, but we did our best. We were crying, but we were also holding up, quietly listening to every word Jonathan said. Whatever he wished or desired, we were present to make it happen.

With tears in my eyes, I ushered out Dr. Chris and Gurjit, thanking them for everything. Taking a deep breath, I pulled myself together before re-entering the bedroom. Immediately, Jonathan exclaimed to Espy, "See, Mama? We can speak openly now, there are no secrets among us, we are a real family now. Everything is in the open, no whispering secretly. I knew about the cancer, Mama. It's just the second part I did not know." By "second part" he was referring to him dying from the cancer. He was not ready to use the word "dying" or "death" yet.

He spoke a lot to us that day. At about five o'clock that evening, when I stepped out of the room for a minute, he very casually asked Espy, "There is nothing you all could do for me, Mama?"

Espy's broken heart shattered. Although I was not there at the time, I felt her pain when she told me. She told Jonathan we had done everything possible and more. Besides all the medical care, we got herbs and made a tea, which he did not like but drank anyway. How we got liver tonics and did not give him meats or processed foods, so that he would get better. But nothing had worked.

"How about a liver transplant? I know Papa was not in favour of that."

"Papa offered to donate part of his liver to you," Espy told him, "but the doctors could not do the transplant because you were jaundiced and too unwell to go through the surgery. Liver transplant is a big surgery, Joddu. And though Papa did not want you to go through this surgery needlessly, he immediately agreed when the doctors told him that a liver transplant was to save your life, and he offered to donate part of his liver to you. But the doctors took you off the transplant list because you were too sick."

"Oh. I did not know that. I know now. It's okay, Mama. Thank you." Even though he had just been told he would die shortly, he did not miss saying "thank you" and "please." I wonder whether I would have been like this in the same situation.

Matthew spent almost all that night with Jonathan. Did the brothers bond? Did they say goodbye? What did they speak about? What did they do? I have not asked Matthew yet.

That night, we all stayed up late and talked. It was as if Jonathan knew he did not have much time with us. We finally slept at about 2:45 a.m., and Jonathan slept soundly. He needed no sleeping medication and had no nightmares. The three nights previous to this, his sleep was disturbed, but after being told that the cancer would end his life, Jonathan slept like a baby, I still find that strange. For the next two days, Jonathan was talkative. Then something changed; he suddenly became quiet and pensive. Though at times he would become slightly worried and ask about his last days, it was out of concern that he not suffer. He didn't want to be in pain and go through complications that needed life-supporting equipment and tubes.

Once, as I sat next to him, he asked me softly, "What will happen in my last days, Papa?"

"I don't know, Joddu." I really did not know. I have not experienced death, and even if I had, how do I answer a question like that from my son?

"I am not afraid of dying," Jonathan continued to my surprise. "I am just worried of the pain or complications or having tubes and pipes in me. I don't want that. I don't want to be a vegetable. Tell the doctors that, please."

"Yes I will, Jonathan. Mama and I will be here all the time. We will do everything to make sure all goes well." Espy and I prayed overtime, asking that his wishes be granted, and we asked relatives and friends to pray, too.

One day, he noticed his feet were swollen. "What is happening, Papa?"

What could I tell him? These were some of the terminal signs we'd been told to expect. Would telling Jonathan lighten his burden? Or will it cause him more pain and anguish? He already knows he is dying. Yet I wanted to speak honestly with him.

"You are going home, Jonathan," I heard myself say gently as he looked at me intently. "Your real home is with "That" which created you. Mama, Matthew and I are just companions assigned to you during your stay on this planet. Your Spirit is your real self. This body you have is like clothing that gets discarded once it is old and useless. In preparation for returning to your real home, Soul or Spirit–You – the real you – is detaching from the body. The body cannot go to the realm of heaven, which is your home. Your home is a fully spiritual realm, and everything is Spirit."

This information was new to me as well as to Jonathan. I had never heard or spoken these words before. "Do you want me to continue, Jonathan?"

Again his big eyes looked at me intently. "A little more, maybe."

"What do you want me to tell you, Joddu?"

He spoke thoughtfully. "Can you tell me about where I am going? And what it will be like?"

How could I? I have not been there, and no one has come back from where he is going and told me what it is like.

"You know a lot, Pa," he whispered with a smile. "I have heard you talking."

"That is not a lot, Jonathan, but I will tell you what I know through my readings and meditations."

He smiled ... a very different smile this time, as if he were saying, "Atta boy, Papa!"

"You see, Jonathan, in your home – the real one – you will meet others who know you. They will be very pleasant and kind. They will know you, but you will have forgotten some of them because you have been away for a long time. God will assign some angels and guides to help you and remind you of the others and of the ways of your home. Everything is good there. You will have all knowledge, you will know everything, and you do not have to learn it."

I paused as he squinted at me. "What do you mean, I don't have to learn?"

"Well, to learn here, you have to read or go to school. At home, it is like an instant transfer of knowledge. You don't have to speak and ask for anything, you just get what you wish."

I recalled how I had received information just before I called back my village friend Felix, then paused to look into Jonathan's Soul, his Shem. There was understanding – he was getting it. He was receptive, receiving this information with no judging, criticizing or challenging. Yeshua's Aramaic words came to mind: *Touveyhoun, lahwvday shlama dawnawhie d'alaha nitqarun* (Divinely attuned and perfectly ripe at this very moment are those who plant God's knowledge; they will be considered instruments of God.)

"I won't be able to talk?" he asked, a little alarmed.

"You won't need to, Jonathan." I was trying more to inform him than to comfort him. "It is a mental communication like an instant download. Everyone knows and everyone gets it instantly. You don't have to explain and don't need explanation. Language was created here on earth by us, but in your real home the language is mental communication." I think he understood what I was trying to convey.

"It seems like a wonderful place. We have been to so many places and so many vacations together, Pa, but now I am going on this wonderful vacation all by myself."

Oh, God! I couldn't take that. But I could not cry; I would not cry. "You remember how much Avozinha loved you, Joddu?"

Jonathan's smile returned. "Yeah, Matthew used to make me ask her for treats and she would never refuse." My mother – Avozinha to Jonathan and Matthew – was possessive of Jonathan and favoured him over her other grandchildren, often unfairly, I thought.

"Yes. She is already there, waiting and preparing for you to arrive. I can tell you for sure, she will not let you feel sad or lost. She will help you."

This seemed to make him happy and settle him a bit, and then he asked, "How about uncle Ramson? He had a similar thing like me, right? Maybe he will help me, too?" Espy's cousin Ramson had passed away about a year earlier from cancer and was also protective of Jonathan.

"Yes, that's true. He loved you very much as well, Joddu, and he and Avozinha got along very well, you remember?" They did. My mum and Ramson would play cards and cheat at the game like little kids.

Not long after this, Espy was helping Jonathan in the washroom, and the conversation turned to his death. Espy mentioned she was afraid of dying.

"Why, Mama? It's no big deal, really."

She was shocked and asked, "Are you not afraid, Joddu?" Her sudden realization that he was not at all afraid made her stop. She told me later that when it struck her that he wasn't afraid, she didn't want to bring him down to the level of her own fear.

Jonathan's reply was casual. "I am not afraid, Mama. What is there to be afraid of? It's no big deal. I will be okay on the other side. Will you be okay?" Espy could not answer him, so he went on, "Don't worry, Mama, I will always be with you."

Later, he spoke to me again. "Papa, I have never eaten junk, hotdogs or any other bad food. What would happen if I had, Pa? Would I still get this?"

"I don't know, Jonathan. We cannot know this, Jod, only God can. Could the cancer have come earlier, later, or not at all? We will never know. You have done everything right. Even the doctors were happy with the way your health had improved. I don't know the answer to your question, Jonathan, but when you are home, you will have this information too." I hope the words were right.

Jonathan replied, "Hm, maybe it was to be."

He asked Espy the same thing. "Why me, Mama? I have never smoked or drunk alcohol or taken drugs. I know some kids my age who do this, and they are okay. I have never even eaten junk food or anything like that, so why is this happening to me?"

"I don't know, Joddu," she said. She didn't; none of us did.

TWENTY-EIGHT

PARTIES AND LAUGHTER

Three days after Jonathan was told he had terminal cancer, he became more pensive. He spoke quietly and thoughtfully, choosing his words carefully. He observed more and was more alert to our feelings. Most importantly, I noticed he had no anger or anxiety. The doctors had prescribed anti-anxiety medications in case of need, but there was no need. On the day he was told of the cancer and that he would die of it, he slept better than he had in the previous three weeks. Earlier, we had to coax him to take either a sleeping pill or melatonin that the doctors had recommended, but now he needed neither and showed no signs of anxiety. I had been worried that his Spirit would be distraught and that we would need to sedate him; this was why I had resisted telling him until it became absolutely necessary. I thank God that he became more at peace rather than anxious.

Elena, the nurse who came in to see Jonathan twice a day, was very caring and dedicated. Every time she arrived, she lifted our spirits, and Jonathan really liked her. Though she knew his prognosis, she wanted to see him feel better. "Jonathan, drink more water," she would say. "Your BP is low today. Eat more, okay?" She was gently nudging him to try and gain strength. One day after she had left, Jonathan called me to sit beside him.

"I know I am dying, Pa. I don't need anybody to remind me things are not working. Can you tell her to just check and make sure I'm okay, that's all?"

I was unnerved by his request but knew that this was the right thing to do. The next morning I met Elena as she entered and asked her to just check him and record the readings, as he had accepted his approaching death.

"He is a child," she said as tears welled. "It is impossible for him to accept. We all want to live."

I related the previous day's conversation with Jonathan.

"He said that?" she exclaimed. "This is not a child. This is a big man! A very big man!" We hugged and cried, and she promised to monitor him, to reassure him, and not to cause him anxiety or worry.

Jonathan noticed the change and enjoyed her visits a great deal. On her day off, he would ask us, "When is Elena coming back? She is the best!" She really was exceptionally good. She cared from the heart and loved Jonathan. Love enabled her to care, understand and know how to provide health care.

I had asked God to tell Jonathan about his time on earth being up. Was this the answer to our prayers? Could it be that Spirit within the body of Jonathan – his real self – received this information from Divine Creator Spirit and had begun preparing Jonathan? To me, this is the only reason Jonathan did not feel anger and was not depressed or needing medication for anxiety and sleeping. As his human senses brought him what Dr. Chris had told him, he let the information go to Spirit for confirmation of what Spirit already knew. I think Jonathan's human senses needed this confirmation so that Spirit could work towards detaching from the body and moving on to the next phase of Spirit's eternal journey.

Jonathan's best friend, Mugzee.

From the human viewpoint, we come into existence through birth and pass away through death. But Spirit is eternal, omnipresent, omniscient, ecstatic, blissful and transcendent. For Spirit, conception, birth and death are merely preparation, entry and exit from this earthly realm.

For the next three weeks and a few days that Jonathan lived among us, often he seemed distant, as if in another world, no longer engaged in the happenings of this place. He became observant, watching Espy, Matthew and me intently. He would observe our dog Mugzee with a naughty smile. I was sad because he was leaving us, but happy he was at peace. That Jonathan was neither anguished nor disturbed brought me great consolation and – dare I say – joy. Yet I was sad beyond consolation. I cried all the time and found dealing with even small matters very difficult. Even though I tried not to cry in Jonathan's presence, he knew I was.

"I know you are crying, Pa." I denied it immediately. "Then why are you sniffing all the time? I know you are crying. You have to accept and let go, Pa. This is how it was to be. You have to accept."

"I will try, Jonathan. I am going to miss you."

"Yes, I know. We have a very special relationship, right? But it will be okay," he assured me.

Jonathan asked us to organize a pasta party with his cousins Erica, Veronica, Ryan, Shannon, and Keane, plus Charbelle, Raquelle and Michelle from India joining us through a Skype video call. They sang for him, did a small play and danced. My sisters Blanche and Jessica organized a "How well do you know Jonathan?" quiz, reminding everyone of funny episodes from his life. It was a good time. Even though Jonathan was finding it painful to laugh, he laughed out loud when Jessica quizzed everyone on what Jonathan's full pet name was. "Joddu Pittul," said Blanche as we all roared in laughter. When he was a baby I had composed a lullaby for Jonathan and the only words in it were Joddu Pittul! Since then this had been Jonathan's official pet name. After the pasta, Jonathan wanted to sleep, and some of the cousins slept in the room with him. He asked me if all his uncles and aunts knew he was dying. I told him we had not told everyone.

Trying to imitate the diver over the waterfall (top right) in Dubai.

"That's okay," he said, "not everyone can handle this. But you must tell Uncle Pat, Uncle Selwyn. They are your cousins, you have to tell them. I want to visit my school, they will start in a few weeks. I would like to go there and meet my teachers and friends. School is my second home. I want to go visit, maybe we will use the wheelchair and go. I would like to see my friends Julian Francis, Nicolas Te, Jinsu Ha, Jordon Ferrazzo, William Barker, Scott Deakin, Iman Shafiei and Brandon Wong."

I talked to Jonathan's school counsellor Ms. Hayhoe, and even though the school year had not begun, she and the vice-principal, Ms. Sabo, came to visit. Jonathan was happy to see them, and they talked about school and discussed arrangements for his friends to visit the week school reopened. Jonathan would have been in grade twelve and looked forward to seeing his friends.

He is saying goodbye. He asked us about people he had not seen recently, friends and relatives who used to come over to our house. He asked about his great-aunt Tia Mila from Kenya, about his godfather and family, about my friends and co-workers.

"They have not come to see me, Pa," he said. That hurt me, and I felt it hurt Jonathan, too. I told him people have busy lives and demanding jobs, so it is not easy for them to visit. He just turned and looked the other way. What was that look? It was almost as if he knew why some people didn't visit him. Why did they not come? When we hear the story of the Good Samaritan, we rightly praise the one who stopped to care for the injured traveller. But how often have we thought of the traveller? What went through his mind as he was being robbed, beaten and left on the side of the road? Did he feel relieved to see a priest approach? And what went on in the priest's mind as he moved to the other side of the road, not giving the injured man a second look? Perhaps the priest was saying to himself, "People are waiting for me to bless the couple getting married today. I cannot make a hundred people wait because of this man. He may have a disease, and I could get infected. Maybe he deserved it, maybe he's a thief who tried to rob someone. Serves him right! God forgive him and look after him. I have to serve the people of God waiting to celebrate the glory of God with me."

As the injured traveller saw the priest hurrying past, did he call out? Or did he stay silent, knowing that the priest did not want to see him? If he called out, would the priest hear and come over? Or would he not hear because he didn't want to?

When Jonathan looked away at my answer, did some of the abandoned traveller's thoughts cross his mind?

Whenever Dr. Chris and Gurjit came to visit, Jonathan was happy to see them.

"How are you doing, Jonathan?" Gurjit asked, her eyes full of tears.

"Fine, thank you."

"Are the medications working well for you?"

"Yes."

"Is there anything you think we can do to help you? Would you like us to arrange a volunteer to come in and play games with you?"

"No, I'm fine. My family is here, and they are doing a great job. They are helping me."

Dr. Chris suggested a counsellor who would speak to Jonathan about God and death if he wanted.

"My dad does a pretty good job of that!" Jonathan smiled and looked at me with his big sparkling eyes. *That is a big compliment from my son, but why am I crying? Why is my heart shattering? This is not how it is supposed to be. My kids are supposed to prepare for my death and funeral, not me for my son's.* The laughter that ensued from Jonathan's comment brought me back. I was determined not to cry. Someone asked Jonathan if I spoke to him about God. "He knows a lot about that," Jonathan said, "maybe too much! If I need to know about God, I will ask my dad. He explains it very well."

Gurjit enjoyed a glass of water while Dr. Chris sipped a coffee. "Jonathan," Dr. Chris said, "we are working on filming a short video featuring kids with terminal diseases. The video is for educational purposes and to help raise funds for PACT, the Paediatric Advanced Care Team at SickKids Hospital. It will be a short twenty-minute video, and we would like to feature you. What do you think?"

Jonathan's face lit up again. "Can I?"

"Of course! We want you to, Jonathan."

"That would be awesome! Yeah! I really want to do it. What do I have to do?"

"Nothing," replied Dr. Chris. "We will come here to your house – that is, if you invite us!" Jonathan grinned. "We will bring our filming crew, and Gurjit and I will talk to you. There is no script that you have to learn or prepare, we'll just talk without a script. And if later there's anything you wish not to be made public, we will edit that out." If Jonathan could have jumped for joy, he would have jumped over the rainbow. Though he could barely walk, the joy and smile on his face were a delight to see. That moment and that smile are imprinted in me forever.

"I want to help others," he said softly. "When I was in the hospital and they inserted the NG tube in my nose, I told my dad I want to volunteer at SickKids and help other kids going through this experience, by talking to them and helping them. My dad also promised to help along with me. I cannot do that now, but I would love to do the video."

"It will be a good legacy for you to leave, Jonathan," said Dr. Chris. They arranged for the filming to be on Wednesday of the following week, which was the twenty-first of August.

That night, Jonathan could hardly contain his excitement as he talked about the video, so we stayed up late with him. "Do I have to prepare, Mama? What should I say? I have never done anything like this. Will they give me a script?" We reassured him that he was in good hands with Dr. Chris – she would guide him and it would not be scripted. "That is the best part," Jonathan said. "If it was scripted, it would be fake. I can't wait for next week! Pap, do you think my awesome couch will come by then? I would like to do the interview sitting in my awesome couch."

TWENTY-NINE

JONATHAN'S AWESOME COUCH

Jonathan's awesome couch! Between the first two visits from the Paediatric Advanced Care Team, we were contacted by the Children's Wish Foundation. Jonathan was offered a wish of something that would make him happy, such as a trip to Disneyland. I told them Jonathan was not able to travel, so the alternative would be computer games or a home theatre system. When I told Jonathan, he was not keen on anything. "I cannot focus on games, Papa. I will hardly play them, and it will just be a waste." Then he thought some more. "Maybe we can get a home theatre system and a couch. I can watch TV on the couch and then it will be for you guys." I went to work on this, but the home theatre system with the couch turned out to be over budget. "Forget the couch," Jonathan said.

"No, Jonathan, I will work to get it within budget for you."

"Please don't start bargaining now, Pa. You're going to do the bargaining thing and tell me how your granddad used to do it. This is not the time for that, okay?" He was interested in a couch that was only sold in home health care stores, and was rather expensive. "That looks so awesome!" he had said. "I would love to watch TV sitting on it."

I was determined to get that couch for him. I searched the internet for better pricing, but to no avail. When I called the manufacturer, they told me they would not sell to an individual. But I wasn't ready to give up. I'm sure they'll sell to Children's Wish Foundation, I thought with excitement. Jonathan saw the sparkle in my eyes. "What did you do, Pa? You are up to something. You are bargaining, right? You cannot do that. You have to buy from the store, they told you so."

"One more day, Jonathan. It will work out."

I conveyed the information to Angela from Children's Wish Foundation, and within a day the manufacturer agreed to sell to the foundation. Jonathan was going to get his awesome couch. Angela told me, "Everything is well within budget. We will try and get everything shipped within a week!"

I ran up the stairs to tell Jonathan the great news. "Joddu, your awesome couch is going to be here for you in a few days. And in the colour you want, too!"

Once again his face lit up, as he grinned, "You are the greatest, Papa, thank you. Crazy – but the best dad I could ever have. I am really going to enjoy the awesome couch. Thank you, Pap." When Espy came into the room shortly after that, I asked Jonathan to tell her the news. "You tell her, you did all the work," he said, but I insisted. "Papa did his Indian tricks," he told her. "Don't know exactly what he did, but they are sending the couch for me." It was such a pleasure to see Jonathan excited about this, his awesome couch. It is still where Jonathan had asked it to be placed – in front of Jonathan's home theatre system. We still call it "Jonathan's awesome couch."

Jonathan on his awesome couch.

THIRTY

SAYING HIS GOODBYES

The next day, we received disappointing news. Dr. Chris had caught the flu and had to cancel the filming scheduled for next week. When I told Jonathan, his face fell. He didn't say a word, he just looked out the window with the same expression as when I'd told him why some of my friends had not come to see him. He'd been so excited to do this. I called PACT back. "Can you reschedule it, please? Jonathan is really looking forward to doing the video." They said that the video and editing were on a tight schedule, and they wouldn't be able to meet their deadline if they rescheduled. Along with Jonathan, I was disappointed, too.

"I really wanted to do the video," Jonathan said. "I hope they come." I called again the next day, but it still could not be done.

Three days later, PACT called us. "We know how much Jonathan wants to be part of this video. Can we come on Thursday the twenty-eighth of August?"

Are you kidding me?! "Of course! Of course!" I will never be able to describe how excited and happy Jonathan was at the news.

"That's next week," he said. "Hopefully my awesome couch will be here by then." By now he was having difficulty walking and trouble balancing. We would help him walk to the washroom or around the bedroom. His energy was low, and he was taking morphine every four hours and sometimes more often. It was obvious to us that even Jonathan knew he would not last much longer. "You guys have done everything for me," he said. "I can never thank you enough. Sorry for giving you so much trouble. I don't know how you do it. I really do not know how you do it. Thank you. Mama, you are absolutely awesome, I am so lucky to have you for my mother. Thank you."

How can anyone respond to that? Espy was crying and so was I when Matthew came in. "How are you doing, Joddu?" he asked.

"Deteriorating," Jonathan replied laconically. Then he asked to be alone with his brother. They talked for some time, and I think Matthew gave him courage. Though Jonathan was not in distress, after speaking to Matthew he seemed better, more serene. At the time, Matthew was reading books on life, God and death. Maybe he told Jonathan some of what he read or knows from Spirit. I feel grateful that Matthew was able to help his younger brother.

When I returned to the room, I again had the feeling that Jonathan was ready to leave. He felt farther away, as if he were partly here and partly somewhere else. When he wanted to talk or say something, he was fully here, but then he would go again. Espy noticed that too. "Why is he like that?"

"He is saying his goodbyes, and it is not an easy thing to do, Espy. Look how hard it is for us to say goodbye to him – and we're saying goodbye to just one person. Jonathan has to say goodbye to all of us, to his cousins, uncles, aunts, friends, teachers, school, games, coaches – the list is sixteen years long. Not only must saying goodbye be very difficult, but having to detach himself from us, his brother and those who have been here with him through his illness is most difficult of all. But he has to detach from us. We cannot take earthly acquisitions and attachments into the kingdom of God. If Spirit cannot detach from these while on earth, Spirit will have to do it later. Let us do all we can to help Jonathan so his Spirit is at peace after leaving the body."

Life and death are not – as we think – opposites of each other. Life is eternal, with no beginning and no end. Birth and death are the entry and exit points of our journey on earth. As we enter earthly existence at birth, Spirit that exists eternally is clothed with a human body from the time of conception. Our bodies and senses have been put together to equip us for our earthly journey. This journey is planned by God, and Spirit is aware of it.

Everything we need for our journey is provided for us. The human cannot sense these things, but Spirit perceives and knows them. After conception, as Spirit is being clothed with the human body, God and Spirit work together to plan events that Spirit is going to have in this human experience.

In Konkani, my mother tongue, the word *nomoskar* is an adaptation of the Sanskrit word *Namaste*. It means *God within me salutes and honours God within you.* Bhagavad Gita says, "He sees truly who sees the Supreme Lord present equally in all."

"The kingdom of God is within you," Yeshua told his friends.

Our existence – our being or our soul – is an expression of God acting through a physical instrument designed by God for God's existence on earth.

THIRTY-ONE

JONATHAN MAKES A VIDEO

"Yeaaaay! They are coming back to do the filming, Pap!" To add to this excitement, Jonathan's awesome couch arrived two hours before Dr. Chris and Gurjit came in with the video team. As soon as the couch – with adjustable back and leg supports – was set up by the technicians, Jonathan asked us to help him to it, and there he waited for Dr. Chris, Gurjit and the team. They were welcomed by a big, big beaming smile. "Hello!" Jonathan said, gesturing proudly. "This is my awesome couch!"

The filming went on for almost two-and-a-half hours, and the raw footage was edited to a seven-minute video available on YouTube (https://www.youtube.com/watch?v=UwGnOBEKIDc).

Dr. Chris Newman (right) and Gurjit Sangha interviewing Jonathan.

Dr. Chris and Gurjit spoke sincerely from the heart with honesty, compassion, empathy, kindness, tears, understanding, and love. They were speaking to Jonathan's Spirit. Jonathan asked direct questions, such as "What should I prepare for? How will it happen? How long from now will it happen?"

To me there was an important question Dr. Chris asked Jonathan: "Your parents decided not to tell you your diagnosis immediately, Jonathan, because they love you very much and did not want to cause you suffering. Do you think they made the right decision?"

He hesitated then smiled and answered, "I think they did the right thing by not telling me. Maybe they could have told me a couple of weeks earlier, but it is good they did not tell me right away. I feel they did the right thing."

Tears again flooded my eyes as I thought, *God! Very few will experience or know the pain I am in because of the approaching death of my son, but I thank you for giving me the wisdom, the strength and the determination to care for your Spirit emanation manifested in our family as Jonathan. Thank you for the knowledge that Spirit is bigger than the body, for teaching me and my family to care for Spirit within Jonathan as well as for his body, when we were told that medicine could do nothing to save him. It is not easy, God. It is the most difficult thing I have ever done. Will I have to do anything more difficult? Please, I hope not.*

After the team left, Jonathan was still excited but also very tired. They had praised and thanked him for doing the video. "Did I really do something good, Papa?" he asked. "They were talking as if I did so much, but I really did nothing. I just talked a bit, listened and answered questions honestly."

"A lot is said without speaking, Jonathan," I said. "They look at you and admire the wisdom with which you speak, the humility and gratitude that flow from you." He seemed confused and asked me how. "Well, just the 'thank you' that you say so often, the 'please' that you say, even though they are here to help you, are things that show others what is in your heart. When I say heart I mean the core of your being – your Soul – or what it is that you are made up of. You are made up of goodness, gratitude, and kindness, and that is very evident. You do not need to say it. People feel it. This is what they admire in you."

"But that is everyone," Jonathan insisted. He asked to rest but did not want to go to bed. "I'd like to sleep on my awesome couch, and then move onto the bed late at night."

As he slept, Espy and I watched over him, and I thought, *Can't he just stay with us? Why does he have to die? Who will benefit from his death? We will look after him, just let him be.* Despite our thoughts and himself knowing he was going to die, Jonathan slept peacefully on his awesome couch.

THIRTY-TWO

GUIDED BY SPIRIT

When we speak of something being "a matter of life and death," we use this physical realm as our frame of reference. But life and death should not be discussed in this way. Life, as we have seen, is eternal – it is Spirit itself. Death, on the other hand, is the disintegration of the form that contained Spirit–Life for a certain window of time. The form that contained Spirit–Life began being manufactured at conception and started functioning in this material earthly realm from birth onwards. It then went through many adaptations, development and growth to finally expire at death. Once "we" die, who is the "we" that lives eternally with God?

As humans, we can only recognize from our own experience. Until we experience death personally, how can we know what death is? Most of us are so afraid of it that we can't even bring ourselves to prepare a will. We work out and eat healthy foods and take medicines to prolong our life. While these are all good to do, we must also accept that we are going to die sometime, no matter what. When we travel, we make an effort to learn a few words of the local language and culture, the places we should see, and so forth. But how many of us want to learn about death and what it will be like when and after we die?

I was no different. I did not want to know. But my journey with Jonathan taught me a little about death and that Spirit – the emanation of God – is the superior power, in continual communion with Creator God. We know that God is Spirit, that the human body is animated by this combination of God and emanating Spirit. And when we realize this, the scales that blind our eyes (and other senses) fall off and we are able to know beyond the senses. We are now truly spiritual, knowing things that the purely human cannot understand; we see things that the purely human cannot see.

When Yeshua spoke of God having hidden the truth from the wise and learned and revealing it to little children, I believe he was speaking of those who let Spirit commune freely and unrestrictedly with God, whatever their ages. As this communion happens, God and Spirit within us are one. There is nothing else that can flow from God except goodness and love. As Spirit in the human becomes one with God, Spirit within us emanates that which flows from God – goodness and love. Is this not a child? The childlikeness referred to by Yeshua is not physical, it is the emanations flowing from us that are the Life, the Truth and the Way to "That" which causes the emanations. *Enana urha shrara wa hayye.*

If we accept our senses as just limited to gathering information, we will be given access and understanding of the vast and eternal information beyond the senses. Sometimes this understanding takes the form of intuition, of a knowing without having learned or studied. This is Spirit receiving information from God. We need to trust and believe that.

The process of humanization, of education and of intelligence-seeking, makes us depend more and more on senses and less and less on Spirit. Unless our senses can confirm something, we do not believe; yet those things that the senses cannot confirm do exist and benefit us. We learn to believe oxygen exists and is all around us, even though we can't detect it with our senses. Who can provide us with the knowledge that Spirit exists and is vital and eternal life?

When the human is able to let go, to be guided by Spirit and not by senses, intelligence and logic, we can say that human has no agenda of itself. Spirit lays down the agenda and unfolds a blueprint that the human just follows. This is truly living by the prompts of the Spirit ... Holy Spirit.

THIRTY-THREE

"AM I HOLDING YOU BACK?"

On the morning after the video interview, Jonathan was almost aloof, quite different from the previous day. He was still excited that he had done the video, but he expressed no desire to see it. He was noticeably weaker and seemed to know it. Again, I felt he was feeling it was time to leave for home. A few times I felt him staring at me, but he turned away when I looked back, so I avoided looking back at him. Was he thinking what I had thought when the doctors told us he had terminal cancer? Did he wonder how long he would be able to see me? I let him look and noticed he looked at Espy, Matthew, Mugzee and others as well. I think he was preparing to say goodbye.

"Are you going to be okay, Pa?" again he asked gently.

My answer was the same as before. "It will not be easy, Joddu, but I promise you I will try to be okay. I am going to miss you a lot." That's all I could say.

"Yeah," he said, "we have a special bond, Pa, but you must not give up. You both have been so good to me. You have done so much for me – you have done everything for me. Brought me the food I like, medicines I need, I don't know how you do it. You are an awesome dad. Awesome, I tell you. Don't forget that. The best ever. I want you to know that. When you think of me, don't think of me in sadness and crying. Be happy, eat some good food and think of me. On my birthday, have a party with some good food and then maybe go to the cemetery and pray for me."

How hard it was to listen to this. Jonathan's seventeenth birthday would be on the twenty-third of December; this was the twenty-ninth of August. "I don't have to go to the cemetery to pray for you, Jonathan," is what I heard myself say.

He looked at me with a knowing understanding. "That's right. You don't have to go anywhere. You can pray from anywhere. But you try your best to be strong, okay?" As I nodded, I felt my heart break. I could not speak. I looked at him, and he held my gaze then slowly turned away.

Soon after that, he spoke to Espy. "Mama, pay attention. You must learn to pay attention and stop this short-term memory loss you have." Jonathan used to tease Espy for her absentmindedness by referring to it as short-term memory loss and compared her to Dory from the movie *Finding Nemo*. "I want you to know that I am so grateful to you. Thank you for all that you have done for me. You guys are awesome. You are awesome, Mama. I couldn't have asked for anyone better to be my mum. You did everything for me. Even woo-doo things like candles, herbs and meditations. I don't know how you do it. It is so difficult. I can see you and Papa struggling to help me to the washroom and other things. But don't be afraid, Mama, I will always be with you. Don't think of me in sadness and crying. Be happy when you think of me. I will always be with you. I will be okay on the other side, Mama. How about you?"

Espy wept. "I'll be okay, Joddu. I'll be okay."

His weakness compared to the previous day was obvious. It was as if he had held himself together for the interview, and now that it was done, he was ready to go home. That evening, he asked me to sit close beside him. "See, Pa," he whispered softly. I could tell it was an effort for him even to speak. "Things are getting difficult. If I feel like coughing, it's difficult, walking is difficult, speaking ... is difficult, ... breathing ... is difficult." I put my arm around him. In my heart, I knew what he wanted to tell me ... I perceived it loud and clear. He wanted to go home; it was too difficult for him to stay. He wanted to tell me that, but he could not bring himself to put it into words, because he knew it would fracture my already broken heart.

"Jonathan, I understand what you are telling me. Do you think I am holding you back, Joddu?"

He gazed at me intently, and that gaze answered my question. Even so, I heard myself say, "What? Am I?"

Jonathan nodded. Very slowly, he said, "Yes, Pa, you are holding me back."

At least now I should have shut up, but "How?" came out of me.

Slowly and softly, Jonathan whispered a reply. "You are crying all the time, Papa. You have to accept and let go. When you do, then everything will be all right."

"Okay, Joddu. I promise to do everything to be strong. But I want you to do something, too." He looked at me curiously. "When you are home," I went on, "I want you not to think of us for some time. You have gone through a lot, you have had so much trouble. I want you to party. Your real family will want to teach you things and enjoy with you. I want you to enjoy, too, for a long time. And then after you have had a good time, you think of us and pray for us, too, okay?"

He nodded with a contented smile. He was present to the situation, with no sadness, no crying, no distress. He was just there. There was still attachment to us, his family, but nothing else seemed of interest to him.

I couldn't believe the words he had spoken. How did such insight come to him? He had never been an overly religious kid, and we had not taught him these things. Could it be that Spirit, which God knows by name – Shem – was taking over the human that we named Jonathan and was recalling things it already knew? The next morning, as we finished breakfast and Espy was going to do her prayers, Jonathan called her to sit beside him.

"What are you praying for, Mama?"

Espy was startled, as he knew what she was praying for and had never asked her this kind of question. "I am asking God to bless you and bless us all, and for complete healing for you."

"No," Jonathan said firmly. "I want you to stop praying for healing." Espy looked at him, bewildered. "I don't want you to pray for healing, Mama. I want you to pray for three things: that I may have no suffering, no pain and no complications." By complications, Jonathan meant life support, with its attendant tubes, wires and machines.

"But Joddu, let me say my prayers!"

"Mama, listen to me. It is difficult for me to speak now. Promise me that you will not pray for my healing. Pray instead that I may not have suffering, pain and complications. Promise me, Mama."

She had to. With tears in her eyes, Espy said, "Okay, Joddu, if that is what you want, I promise."

"I want you to tell all your friends to do the same, too."

"Okay," said Espy.

I was there too, and he turned to me. "You heard, Pa?"

"Yes, Joddu, I heard."

After a few minutes, Espy got up and headed to the next room to pray. Jonathan called after her, "You remember what you promised me, Mama?" almost as a teacher would ask a student. Espy assured him she did. "None of that short-term memory Dory stuff, okay?" They smiled at each other. He was telling her he was going home, that he wanted her prayers to help him clear some of the difficulties on the remainder of his journey on earth. How hard for a mother to hear her child say this. How can a mother listen to her sixteen-year-old ask her to help him die well? Espy, like Jonathan, had to be present, hold his hand, put her arm around him, let him rest his head on her shoulder, and do all this knowing that he was moving on and going home.

As Jonathan drifted off to sleep, Espy asked me, "What is he saying? Why is he saying that?"

"What can I say to you, Espy? I don't know what to say. This is what we have to go through." She stared at me. We were both crying but keeping it quiet so as not to wake or alarm Jonathan.

When Matthew came in to spend some time with Jonathan, I called my sisters and told them of Jonathan's prayer request.

"My God, is that what he is saying?" Jessica said from her home in India. "I am going to look for flights to come there." I insisted she didn't, as her children are young and still in school. "How are we going to do this, Vincent?" she cried out.

"I don't know, but we have to. We are not given a choice. Somehow, we have to."

Jessica agreed to pray as Jonathan had asked. I called Angelo, Brian, Blanche, Raymond, and Narcissa. Espy called Ana and Yvette and told them the same thing.

"No, we will storm heaven for him," Brian, my schoolmate from Calangute, insisted. "He is just a child. He is just a child ... man!"

I waited until Brian was calmer, then explained, "Jonathan is at peace, dear friend. He is okay. He has told us he will be 'okay on the other side.' He hopes only for the three things he asked us to pray for: no pain, no suffering, and no complications. You will not believe me, Brian, but he is in no distress at all. Rather, he is almost fused with God. He is very different. He not only knows where he is going, I think he is already there."

Brian was in tears as he took this in. "I will honour his wishes, Vincent. I will tell my family and the others here as well to honour Jonathan's wishes."

On the thirtieth of August, Jonathan appeared a little brighter. His eyes were clearer, but his motor functions were more diminished. We asked for a hospital bed to be brought to the house, and Jonathan was excited, which to me seemed strange and sad. But he was really happy, excited and impatient to try it out as soon as it arrived. "I do not want to go to the hospital again. I just want to go to sleep and not wake up. That's it."

He could see that Espy and I were feeling the strain. As he sat on the bed after we had helped him back from the washroom, he shook his head as if to say, "No, this is not right."

Thinking he was uncomfortable I said, "What is it, Joddu?"

The sadness in his beautiful eyes pained me. "You guys are struggling. I know it's difficult for you. I don't know how you do this. I don't know how you manage. Thank you, Mama ... Papa, thank you." Neither Espy nor I could say anything. "Maybe you should talk to Dr. Chris about me going to the hospice."

"But, Joddu, you want to be home, right?" Espy said.

"Yes, but not if it is so difficult for you guys." I could not speak.

"Joddu, look, you don't worry about that," Espy continued. "We are here for you. Papa and I will do anything and everything. We can manage, even if we fight among ourselves – you don't worry about that. We fight because each one of us wants to do the best for you. We have our own ways, but we will do this. We love you and that will never change. We are not forced to do this for you, Joddu. No one forced us. What we are doing is out of love for you. And love is always right, Joddu. Whatever we have to do we will do, and it will always be right, because we love you. If we cannot, then we will consider the hospice. Okay?"

"You promise you will consider if it gets difficult?" Jonathan looked at me as he answered Espy.

"Yes," we both replied. He seemed reassured. Again, I was delighted to see that he was not in turmoil. It was as if he had achieved equilibrium.

In the last days of his life, Jonathan was not Jonathan. He was an observer of everything, from his failing body to all the things we said and did. Sometimes he would smile weakly at our words and actions, and at other times his normal sarcastic remarks would resurface. Who was this "he" that was different from the Jonathan we knew so well? It was Spirit, that which entered this earthly realm on the twenty-third of December 1997 and we named Jonathan. That which was observing now is what existed, exists and forever will: *tat sat Atma* ("that true Spirit").

A little later that day, I was worried and asked, "Jonathan, are you okay?"

He looked at me, puzzled. "What do you mean?"

"I don't know, do you want me to do anything?"

He shook his head. "Nope."

Still not satisfied, I asked, "Do you want me to talk to you about God?"

Very gently he answered, "No, he is right here inside me." I was stunned, and Jonathan saw the shock in me. "God is inside me, Papa ... helping me," he said with difficulty. "It's going to be okay." His face, his eyes, his demeanor told me more than the words he spoke. He was already home. Jonathan was still alive, but it was plain he not only knew where he was going, he was already there. The strangeness of it strikes me even now, that he was still among us and Spirit had not left the body of Jonathan, yet he was already in the realm we call his true home. How delightful for him; and how very, very sad it felt for us.

That evening, I had another fight with God when I sat for my meditation. "How can you make him suffer like this?" I demanded. "What has he done? If it was me, than do what you have to do, and dispose of me as you wish. But to make my son suffer because of an issue you have with me or him is – by your own definition – cowardice. Jonathan has accepted his approaching death, he has prepared himself, he has said his goodbyes, he is at peace with going home, and he has even asked you to take him. Why then are you torturing my boy? What is it that you are gaining by doing this? Can't you see he is suffering? That he is ready and prepared to go home? Why are you delaying and making him suffer all the more?" Of course, no booming voice replied. There was just silence. Maybe, like us, God did not want to disturb God's child in the next room.

THIRTY-FOUR

"I'M DONE"

On the first of September, Jonathan asked me to let him be alone for some time. I felt that was strange, as he needed someone with him all the time to help him or just keep him company. "I want to talk to God. I'll call you when I'm done."

I handed him the call button and left. About twenty minutes later he called, and I sprinted back. As I walked in, I looked at him, and something told me to stay silent. He was calm, assured and very much at peace. He looked back at me, and that was enough communication for both of us. I didn't ask and he didn't say how his "talk with God" had gone. We both knew. Jonathan was fine. He was home.

Later, as Espy helped him eat, he said, "Mama, if I sleep and do not wake up, let this be my goodbye for you."

Espy told me she could not keep herself from saying, "Why are you saying that, Joddu? Everything will be okay."

By that evening, Jonathan's physical condition had deteriorated drastically. He became very weak and quiet and was having difficulty breathing and speaking. He asked for a notepad and pencil. Slowly, very slowly, he wrote, and indicated to Espy to read what he had written:

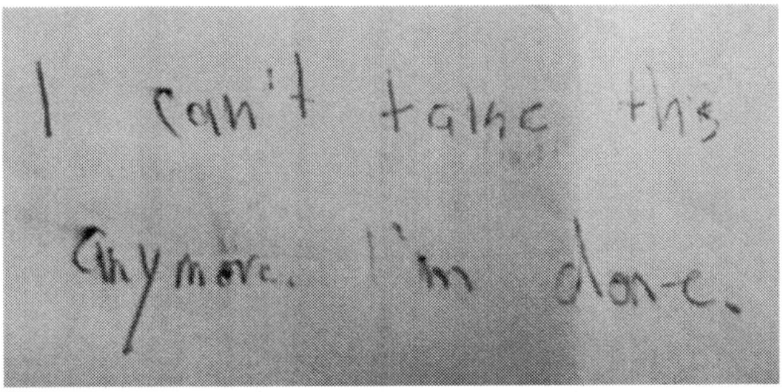

What was it he couldn't take anymore? Was he making an effort to stay long enough to see us through the process of acceptance? Was this effort what was causing him suffering? Was it difficult for Jonathan's Spirit to stay in the body now that his time to be in the body was up?

Today, when I look back, I know that Jonathan accepted his approaching death almost immediately after he was told that his illness was terminal. I think full acceptance came to him three days after Dr. Chris Newman told him of his prognosis. After that, he began preparing for the final part of his earthly sojourn. More importantly, he was trying to help Matthew, Espy and me come to a place of accepting the will of God. He wanted assurance within himself that we were going to be all right. He had told Espy, "Mama, I will be okay on the other side. Will you be okay?" He also told her, "I will always be with you."

Two days later, Jonathan called his uncle Proto to his side and asked him to write out a note he wanted us to send to Dr. Eberhard at SickKids. This is what the note read: "*I never had a doctor that was there for me as much as you were. You treated me more as a friend in need, rather than just another patient, cause you comforted me when I broke down and came to St. Michael's (hospital) and were there for all my ordeals. I am very glad that I was under your care. Thank you for everything. – Jonathan.*" (Jonathan had been at St. Michael's for a procedure that wasn't available at SickKids.) Proto wrote this on a thank-you card after Jonathan was home and I delivered it to the desk of Dr. Eberhard at SickKids Hospital.

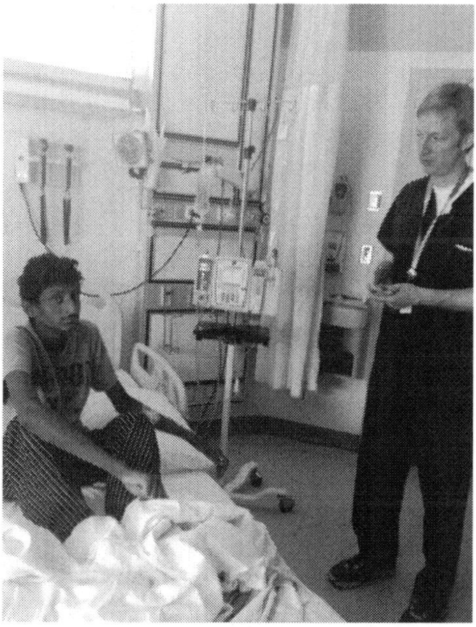

Dr. Eberhard talking to Jonathan in his room at SickKids Hospital, Toronto.

An ancient Indian saying tells us, "When men takes one step towards God, God takes seven steps towards men." Taking a step towards God is difficult, because we are raised to be independent and stand on our own two feet. Most of us are not raised to rely on Spirit. We depend instead on our senses, logic and intelligence, which are instruments of Spirit and which often stand as road blocks to Spirit.

Reminding ourselves that reality lies beyond the senses is the first step towards God. Realizing that God and Spirit are as one, in communion within us, is the second step. And so our steps continue, one after the other, until we arrive in the kingdom of God. When Spirit is one with God and in charge of the human, every thought, word and deed flows from God – the source of Spirit. How can that ever be wrong? This is why it is said, "When we act from the heart, it is always out of love and it is always good." God acts from love. We can, too, if we take that first step.

God is the essence of love, kindness, compassion, empathy, joy, and pure divinity, and God is within us. "If the one who leads you should say to you, 'See the kingdom is in heaven,' then the birds of heaven shall precede you. If they say to you, 'It is in the sea,' then the fish will precede you. But the kingdom is inside of you and outside of you. When you know yourselves, then you will become known, and you will understand that you are the sons of the living father. But if you do not know yourselves, you dwell in poverty and it is you who are that poverty." – The Gospel of Thomas, saying 3.

"That which is within tells me the nature of everything."
~ Lao-Tzu (Tao TeChing)

THIRTY-FIVE

COUNTING BREATHS

When a person dies, we often say they gave up the spirit. But this is not the case, it is the other way around. Spirit, being eternal and greater than the body, gives up the body.

Over the next few days, Jonathan asked about all his relatives. And we had parties – a pizza party, a cousins' party, a birthday party for Raymond, and an Indian food party. Throughout these, Jonathan was tired but stayed up. His body was failing, and Spirit now clearly wanted to go home. Raymond and Narcissa had been planning to celebrate Raymond's birthday with a trip to Montreal, but they cancelled their plans to spend it with Jonathan. Raymond brought in Jonathan's favourite Italian food, and we ate in the bedroom with him. Although he ate little, he enjoyed what he did eat. Then Jonathan called Raymond close to him and handed him a greeting card with a small gift certificate. "This is only for you and Narcissa, don't give it to anyone else." We ate the Indian food by sitting on mats on the floor. Jonathan was grinning at this; he could not laugh out loud by now.

In the afternoon of the fourth of September, Espy wanted to go to the store, but Jonathan asked her not to. "Why do you need to go now?" Espy explained she needed to pick up a few things and would be back in an hour. "Okay," he said. "Come back soon, okay? Don't get distracted." That naughty, teasing smile showed up as Espy promised not to.

As she drove home, she prayed, "God, my Jonathan is suffering. I cannot see him like this. If it is your will that he should die, then I accept your will. I pray that he may not have pain, may not suffer and that he may have no more complications. This my prayer is as he wishes, and though I want him to be healed, I let go of my wishes, my wants and my desires. In doing so, I pray for peace, for divine healing for Jonathan and all of us. I let go of clinging to him. If this is your will, please take Jonathan and please also help us walk this journey. Give us all the strength to let go and trust. I know all will be well."

As soon as Espy walked into the bedroom, I knew she'd been crying, but I didn't want to say anything in Jonathan's presence. He was very happy to see her back so quickly. A short while later, his big-screen TV arrived, courtesy of the Children's Wish Foundation. Proto, who was staying with us, and I got to work assembling the table and getting it connected. Jonathan was sitting in his awesome couch watching TV on the old set, and when we asked for a half-hour break to remove the old TV and hook up the new one, he was pretty excited. "Can I watch you guys?" We set up the TV stand and connected the wires, then got the TV out of the box. "Wow!" he said.

Shortly after everything was connected, his cousins Shannon and Keane came to visit. They watched TV and ate dinner with us. At about 9:00 p.m., Jonathan said he was tired and wanted just Espy and me in the room. Shannon and Keane said their goodbyes and left for the night. I noticed Jonathan was very quiet and observant as they left.

He had eaten nothing. We tried to feed him his favourite cookie, but after a bite or two he said he'd had enough. "I'm done."

We helped him onto his hospital bed and moved it so it was right next to Espy, who slept on our bed. From there she would lovingly hold his hand and pray herself to whatever sleep she could grab. At 10:45 as I lay down on the other side of our bed, Jonathan said, "I'm feeling dizzy."

In a flash I was up and beside him. "Do you want to sit up?" Yes, he did. Espy and I supported him, one on each side, to help him sit up. "You have not eaten anything, Jonathan. Do you want me to get you something?"

"I cannot eat, Pa."

What could I do to make him feel better? How could I comfort him? "How about some watermelon juice?" He liked watermelon.

"Okay." I rushed downstairs to pour fresh watermelon juice that Espy had prepared, and I couldn't resist bringing a cookie as well. Jonathan smiled slightly as I came back, as if to say, "I knew you would get something else." As I sat beside him, Espy helped him take a couple of sips of watermelon juice. I think he had two tiny bites of the cookie as well. "Soothe me, Mama," he said quietly as he rested his head on Espy's shoulder. She was exhausted. She hadn't slept for more than a couple of hours a night in months, yet she held up for her dying son.

Espy cutting her 50th birthday cake with Jonathan.

We sat there with him. He asked for a piece of Airheads (now his favourite candy), the blue one. It wasn't available where we lived, but Raymond and Narcissa had brought him some from Toronto. "Just a small piece," he said. We sat this way and talked till about 3:00 a.m., when he started to look sleepy.

"Do you want to lie down, Jod?" I asked.

"I think so." Gently, very gently, Espy and I helped him lie down. Espy lay on our bed beside him, and I turned off the light. In the glow of the night light I saw Jonathan so calm and restful. I raised my hand in blessing as I walked to the other side and lay down.

"Vincent, Jonathan did not ask for anything all night," I heard Espy say. I bolted out of bed and was beside Jonathan. He was still calm and resting, but breathing slowly – too slowly, I felt. "Count the breaths," a voice seemed to tell me. I counted: seventeen breaths to the minute at 8:15 a.m. I washed up and was back in two minutes to count again: fourteen breaths to the minute. I woke up Espy and asked her to call Matthew, who was on his way to work but turned around immediately. Somehow I knew. I was experiencing Spirit's final moments on earth in the form of Jonathan. I knelt on Jonathan's left side, held his hand and placed it on my left cheek as I used to when he was a baby.

"Joddu," I said, "I am right here beside you. I know you can hear me. I love you very much, I am right here." A tear rolled from his left eye. I wiped his tear, crying silently so Jonathan would not hear me. Espy knelt down on the other side of the bed, speaking very gently to him, and another tear rolled from his other eye.

I called Dr. Berger, the visiting doctor for Jonathan, the minute his office opened. "What should I be doing?" I asked the nurse who answered.

Matthew and Jonathan Leitao – Spring 2013.

"Just do what you are doing and what you have been doing." Her voice was calm, kind and very comforting. "Just be with him. Hold his hand, talk kindly to him. Count his breaths if you wish. I think you and your family have been absolutely wonderful, loving and selfless. Jonathan is blessed to have you for his family. Gather your family around. He is passing away. Keep talking to Jonathan – he can hear you. We wish you all the best, we pray for you, and we love you all. The doctor is not in yet, but I'll call him, and he'll be on his way shortly."

Proto and Espy were still at Jonathan's bedside when I went back in. Ana, Espy's sister, had also come over. A supervisor nurse had arrived as well to ensure Jonathan was getting the care he needed. Maria, our family helper, came in to sit beside Jonathan; she had cared for him and seen him grow from the age of six. Espy's eighty-five-year-old mum, who lives with us and whom Jonathan called Mai, walked to the room with great difficulty. Matthew arrived from his way to work and asked us to give him some time alone with Jonathan. For a long time, just the two brothers were in the room with the door closed. Soon after Matthew let us all in, Narcissa arrived from work. It was now about 11:00 a.m. We all were by the bedside, praying, and as if not to be left out, Mugzee our American bulldog (and Jonathan's best friend) came in and found himself a spot at Jonathan's bedside.

Usually when he comes upstairs to our room, Mugzee rolls about on the carpet as if he is making snow angels, which would make Jonathan laugh. This time was different. As we sat or knelt around Jonathan's bed, Mugzee sat with us and gazed at Jonathan as if to say, "I am here too, Jonathan." He did not bark or howl, he just sat there and gazed.

I called my sisters, my cousin Father Patrick, Allan, and as many others as I could remember. "Please pray for Jonathan and us," I said. "Jonathan is dying." At 12:15 p.m. on the fifth of September 2014, my dear son took his last breath, and Spirit left Jonathan.

For me, everything became still. Then in the stillness, I heard, "He is not breathing." Just as I became aware that those words had been mine, I heard Espy call out to Jonathan, then Ana called out, then Mai. Then I heard weeping, and realized my face was wet with tears. I hadn't heard myself cry until that moment. *Jonathan,* my heart was saying in silence, *peace be with you. Peace, love and joy be with you forever. I love you.*

THIRTY-SIX

"WHAT IS THE TASTE OF THIS GRAPE THAT I EAT?"

To live, Spirit depends not on the body, but on God. Without Spirit, the body cannot see, speak, hear, taste or walk around. Spirit had just left Jonathan's body, and the body was devoid of all human activity.

As a boy, I heard preachers preach from pulpits, altars and platforms, and now I have acquired friends and relatives who tell me, "You have to accept God's will," or "The Lord is so wonderful and has great plans for you." How can I accept what I do not know? In human terms, to not know is to not see, hear, smell, touch or taste. How can I eat something that I cannot see, hear, smell, touch or taste? Not knowing is being blind, and accepting without knowing is as foolish as trying to eat something that we cannot see, touch, smell, taste or hear. Someone telling us to accept without knowing is one blind person leading another.

We have to realize the inevitability of each and every moment, and know that God's plan is being revealed to us moment by moment. It is not in the past or the future, it is in the present moment. By accepting inevitability of this moment, we live in the current moment. As we live in the moment that God is revealing to us, the human is "being" in God's plan as it unfolds. Only after knowledge can acceptance happen.

Divine and Spiritual Knowledge cannot be acquired, gathered, sought or found. It can only be experienced. A woman asked Yeshua to let her sons sit at either side of him. Yeshua replied, "You don't know what you are asking. Are you able to drink the cup I am about to drink?" The only way we can know what the human senses cannot validate is if the source of all knowledge gives that knowledge to that true Spirit which is within us.

My mind wanders to India. I see an ascetic Hindu saint walking from village to village, blessing all those he meets. Villagers give him food and let him rest and sleep in the local temple before he walks on to the next village. His story is that, a long time ago while he was working in the field, a gang of robbers attacked his village, raided his home and killed the saint's wife and two children. He never speaks of it; he just goes from village to village, offering blessings to anyone and everyone.

One day an orphan boy shares a meal with the saint, who feels compelled to share his story with the boy. "I know how you feel, swamiji," the boy says. "My father died a few years ago, and I feel very sad when I think of him."

The saint smiles, looks up, and sees a bunch of ripe grapes. He plucks a few and says to the boy, "Have you ever eaten grapes?"

"Of course, swamiji, I have eaten grapes of this very vine often."

Again the saint smiles as he puts a grape into his mouth and starts eating. "So tell me, young sahib, what is the taste of this grape that I eat?" The young boy looks at the saint. He is startled and surprised, then bewildered. With his lips, he tries to form words, then tears roll down his dusty cheeks. As he sits sharing a meal with the saint, his only response is silence.

THIRTY-SEVEN

SPIRITS INTERTWINED

In my village, a friend had a grapevine growing in the yard. It was a robust plant, thriving on very little care and producing a lot of grapes. Besides eating the grapes, I would often just look at the vine, its branches intertwining and crisscrossing like the mouth of a river. Certain branches particularly interested me. They stemmed from the main vine, but as they touched each other in the maze of branches, they fused together at the point of contact, then went their individual ways to bear fruit. As a child, I wondered if this fusing was a defect in the mother vine or a defect at the point of contact. I tried to pry apart the two branches, but the bond was too strong.

Now I wonder, if I had been able to pry them apart, would it have hurt the vine? Would the plant have felt pain? My human self can't know what the grapevine would have felt, but I know firsthand the pain of having Jonathan pried apart from my human existence and experience. My son's death feels like a prying apart of an intrinsic and primordial part of me, with two distinct components. There's the physical and human separation of Jonathan from me, his human dad, and there's a resultant delusion of the spiritual separation of Spirit (Jonathan's) from Spirit (mine). The pain of losing my child is beyond human senses, beyond this earth. The void and emptiness in my being, the feeling of being flayed, is as fresh now as when we were first told Jonathan's prognosis. Yet my pain is not physical. Unlike Jonathan in the x-ray room, I am not experiencing physical pain, but like him my Spirit is confused, deluded and in pain. Many cannot see this; they have eyes only for the material, the physical and the tangible. Only those in tune with Spirit can "know" this.

In the human realm – let's call it the realm of the senses – understanding comes after knowing, and knowing comes after experiencing. In Spirit, where there are no limiting forms or boundaries, one fuses with all, and especially with loved ones, to experience life events of the other. This is why I experienced and saw Jonathan's pain and anguish in the x-ray room. As Jonathan's human dad, I saw him in pain and heard him cry out for help. But Spirit within me experienced the pain that Spirit within Jonathan was experiencing. The only way to experience in this way is by fusing with Spirit in the other, just like the vine branches. When this happens, then knowledge, understanding, compassion and empathy all flow from Spirit. And the only way to achieve this is through Divine and unconditional love. Through Divine Love we are all connected to each other and to our Source the Creator.

As humans, we attempt to clothe ourselves with knowledge, understanding and communication but miss the main ingredient of Love. But if we remember that the human is a garment of Spirit, we will see that all human qualities, including human understanding, are like the colours and designs adorning a garment. This is why Yeshua referred to Pharisees – who were doing their job – as *apae* (mask). Their actions originated from the covering, not from the core of Spirit. Understanding needs to emanate from a knowing in our hearts, from Spirit or Shem. Only then is it as real as Spirit itself.

Even though I know this, my human self continues to look to the senses for confirmation of Jonathan's existence. But he is no longer in the realm of the senses. He is in the realm of Spirit – the kingdom of God – and that is where I will find him. This all-too-human seeking of my beloved Jonathan in the realm of the senses leads Spirit astray.

Enana urha shrara wa hayye. The "I" within "I" is the way, the truth and the life.

Jonathan and I are both emanations from God. We came physically together at Jonathan's birth, animated different material bodies, but like the branches of the grapevine, our nourishment and its source are the same. Now, though his physical body is no more, Spirit that was in his body lives eternally in the kingdom of God. "The kingdom of God is within you," Yeshua told us. So within me is the kingdom of God, and that is where Spirit is: the same Spirit that is me (Enana) and is Jonathan (Enana).

What is truly real is that which is in the kingdom of God – the Divine Source of all Love and Knowledge from which we all emanate. If, instead of reaching out through our senses, we were to reach within to Enana, Soul, Spirit, Atma or Shem, what would we find? Would we find the kingdom of God that Yeshua said is within us? Instead of reaching out through the senses, can we travel back to the heart of us, to the Source of all Love and Knowledge? And, if we do, what will we find?

I find not only my Source, but the Source of all. I find that we are all one and that all live for the benefit of one other. I find that Jonathan lives and so do I, because there is not just a "Jonathan" and a "me," there is us all. The separation from Jonathan that I experience is a delusion caused by the inability of the senses to bring in data or information from beyond the realm of the senses. This delusion is only present in the realm of the senses and non-existent in the kingdom of God. When I am in communion with God, I am not in pain; but when I am in the realm of the senses, I am in humanly unimaginable pain from the loss of my son.

To solve a problem, we need a different way of thinking from that which caused it. So how can the human experience that deludes me into feeling a separation from Jonathan help me overcome it? Can the human, with its protocol, logic and technology that are gone in a blink of an eye, heal the wounds of eternal Spirit?

Just as God planned this earthly sojourn for Jonathan and gently let him know when it was time to return home, so also God causes to heal that which seems shredded. If Spirit stays in continual communion with God, then God and Spirit are as one within us, just as Spirit within Jonathan was one with God even before his human death. "God is inside me, Papa ... helping me," Jonathan said.

Whatever made me say "Spirit is bigger than the body" was not my human self. It had to be the other "me" in me – Enana or Shem – taking control and sounding the words through my vocal cords during the erosion of Jonathan's body.

So Shem within must have been in control at least some of the time, even though Vince – the human instrument – was often in control. Did not Vince want to pull a gun on God? This person called Vince needs to become less and less, so that Shem can become greater and greater. As that happens, I know Jonathan and I are still together in the kingdom of God within me.

In his last days, Jonathan hardly functioned and could barely use his human motor abilities. At the same time, Shem was so great, it was obvious to anyone with eyes to see that Shem was already home with God.

Will the Shem that manifested and dwelt among my family as Jonathan know the Shem within me when I go home? Will Shem know Shem? Do they need to, or are they the same?

Shem *Shem*

~~Jonathan~~, do you know ~~me~~?

Suggested Reading

Cayce, Edgar (1988). *Channeling Your Higher Self* (audio book).

Chopra, Deepak (2008). *The Third Jesus.* New York, NY: Three Rivers Press.

DuBois, Allison (2007). *We are Their Heaven.* New York, NY: Fireside.

Emoto, Masaru (2004). *The Hidden Messages in Water.* Hillsboro, OR: Beyond Words Publishing.

Long, Jeffrey, and Perry, Paul (2010). *Evidence of the Afterlife.* New York, NY: HarperOne.

Holland, John (2011). *Messages from the Other Side.* A.R.E. Press (audio book).

Holmes, Ernest, and Kinnear, Willis (1999). *Thoughts are Things.* Deerfield Beach, FL: HCIBooks.com.

Kübler-Ross, Elisabeth (1969). *On Death and Dying.* New York, NY: Scribner.

Leadbeater, Charles. W. (2010). *Invisible Helpers.* New Orleans, LA: Cornerstone.

Moorjani, Anita (2012). *Dying to Be Me.* Carlsbad, CA: Hay House.

Morash, Shari (2014). *Loving Your Baby.* Guelph, ON: Shari Morash.

Nagel, Avril, and Clark, Randie (2012). *When Your Child Dies.* Far Hills, NJ: New Horizon Press.

Piper, Don, and Murphey, Cecil (2004). *90 Minutes in Heaven.* Grand Rapids, MI: Revell.

Teilhard de Chardin, Pierre (1975). *The Phenomenon of Man.* New York, NY: HarperCollins.

Tolle, Eckhart (2004). *What is Meditation?* (audio book).

Yogananda, Paramhansa (1946). *Autobiography of a Yogi.* New York, NY: Philosophical Library.

Suggested Viewing

Being in Heaven
The Big Question
Conversations Beyond Proof of Heaven
Flight from Death: The Quest for Immortality
Heaven is for Real

Other Helpful Resources for Bereaved Parents

Child Bereavement UK: Information sheets (support for adults)
http://www.childbereavementuk.org/publications/information-sheets/

SickKids: Helping Yourself with Grief
http://www.sickkids.ca/ProgramsandServices/paediatric-advance-care-team/Grief%20and%20bereavement%20resources/griefwords-library/GriefWords-Library.html

31813654R00124

Made in the USA
Middletown, DE
13 May 2016